THE BABY
BEDTIME
BOOK

THE BABY
BEDTIME
BOOK

Say
Goodnight
to
**Sleepless
Nights**

Fi Star-Stone

The views in this book are those of the author but they are general views only and readers are urged to consult the relevant and qualified specialist for individual advice in particular situations.
G2 Entertainment Limited hereby exclude all liability to the extent permitted by law of any errors or omissions in this book and for any loss, damage or expense (whether direct or indirect) suffered by a third party relying on any information contained in this book.

All our best endeavours have been made to secure copyright clearance for every photograph used but in the event of any copyright owner being overlooked please address correspondence to G2 Entertainment Limited, Unit 7-8, Whiffens Farm, Clement Street, Hextable, Kent BR8 7PQ.

To my wonderful friends, my fabulous followers and my fantastic family – in particular my supportive husband Richard, my parents and my two wonderful children Betsy and Oscar. Thank you for your incredible support and belief in me and my book.

This book is also dedicated to all of the wonderful children and parents I have worked with over the years, but in particular to two very special little boys and their parents, Jack, Ben, Karen and James.

And finally thank you – to you the reader for trusting in me to help you say goodnight to sleepless nights! Let your journey begin...

Thank you for trusting me and thanks to everyone who contributed to the book! #SayGoodnight2SleeplessNights

CONTENTS

FOREWORD

BY ALEX WINTERS

The Baby Bedtime book really is a must for parents. Whether you're a first time parent or like me enjoying your third child, there is so much you can take from Fi's words of wisdom. What I really appreciate about the book is that at no time do I feel patronised or feel like I'm a useless parent. The advice is realistic and supportive. The real beauty about this book is that it has actually helped me with my own child. Success!

PREFACE

EVERYONE IS DIFFERENT

When I qualified as a nursery nurse in 1993 and began my first job as a Nanny, I was incredibly happy. I'd worked hard for two years, studying for my NNEB and enjoyed the experiences provided by my training placements in hospitals, schools, nurseries and family homes. I was so excited to put everything I had learned into practice.

From that first job to the hundreds of children I cared for as a nanny and nursery nurse, child after child reinforced the conviction that I had chosen the right career. Every day of my working life was fun and every day was educational. My training helped me develop techniques and routines that I shared with other parents and nannies and their responses inspired me to set up a blog.

That blog eventually became the web site Childcare is Fun and those techniques and routines are the ones you are about to read about in this book.

My interest in child development and the changes in childcare methods led me to the Open University, where I studied for a degree in Childhood and Youth Studies while continuing to work full time.

Holding down an 8am to 6pm nannying job and a part time University degree course was pretty hard going. But I was dedicated and committed and so I gained my degree and a vast amount of extra knowledge along the way.

Becoming a parent for the first time in 2009 was a powerful blow to my emotional circuit board. All my ideas of parenthood floated out of the window together with my child free years.

Don't get me wrong, the first few days of being a mum were fantastic. My beautiful baby slept like a dream, breastfed perfectly and life was sweet. This motherhood malarkey was easy. Or so I thought.

Then my little newborn showed me what crying in the early hours with reflux was all about. Like most parents I had to manage on little sleep. My daughter taught me that parenting wasn't anything like nannying or teaching or caring for other people's children. Parenting was a whole different ball game!

Although I had all my training and experience behind me nothing had prepared me for the super-shock of having my own child. It was this experience, above all others, that made me realise how valuable my techniques, and the advice I had given to other parents, really was.

Learning how to function on little sleep, learning how to comfort a colicky, refluxy baby, learning how to enjoy the entire process. Putting new ideas into practice on my baby that worked and then sharing those ideas.

It was then that it hit me how terribly frightening and overwhelming parenthood must be to Mums and Dads with no experience of looking after little ones. Being thrust into a childcare world of feeding, nappies and sleepless nights must be overwhelming.

I decided to help by opening a free parenting advice service. It became so popular that I was asked over and over again to write a book. Mums and Dads wanted me to share the techniques that help parents and babies get that most magical and elusive of things; sleep.

As the over tiredness crept into my own life I realised that I needed to use the techniques that I'd used on hundreds of other little ones to create happy daily routines and a happy bedtime baby sleeper for myself!

My baby needed me to put my tried and tested, gentle techniques into practice. And so I did.

I began my journey into parenthood. I was happier and calmer and sleep deprivation only came when childhood illness, particularly on our case reflux, came as well.

My two little ones were, and still are, happy bedtime baby sleepers. And so I share with you my easy to follow, simple routines and techniques to help you say goodnight to sleepless nights and join me in a happy parenting journey.

Far from magic

Many of the parents using the parent advice service on my web site have that I'm magical. They've said that my ideas and calm ways have cast a spell over their family.

I assure you that my techniques and ideas are not magical, or spellbinding. There's no wand in my pocket and I don't wear pointy fairy shoes - I wear Converse. I use simple strategies that have been tried and tested over 20 years during my career. And they work. They really work.

I help parents to develop confidence and happiness in their parenting. It's not easy becoming a parent and yet it's not totally dreadful.

Yes there are sleepless nights when the children are poorly. And those nights are accepted as sleepless - but you can have a happy bedtime baby on all the other nights, and from a very young age, by following my simple, gentle, techniques.

Before we go any further on our happy bedtime baby journey, I thought I'd tell you about a couple of lovely stories from two parents who have kindly let me share with you their experiences.

They've both used the parent advice service. I'd love to have shared more, but I think that would be another book in itself – with over 150 emails received each week I could probably fill and encyclopaedia of parenting problems!

I've chosen these parents in particular because they were all experienced Mums and Dads who already had children but needed help with the different behaviour they encountered when they became parents again. This highlights that all babies and children are different. Your first child may be a perfect, happy bedtime baby sleeper, but your second might not.

I think by sharing these two examples with you, you'll see that this guide can help any parent struggling with unhappy sleepers, not just first time, brand-new parents.

Sam's story

Karin, a mum of two, came to me when her youngest, Sam, wasn't sleeping. This is what she had to say:

"Fi is a well-known expert in all things baby and when we were struggling with our son Sam, and at our wit's end, I knew, if Fi had the time, she could help us. At 21 months, Sam had given us several weeks of rubbish sleep and we were suffering as a family as a result.

"After a fairly consistent and normal bath and bedtime routine, Sam would sleep decently from eight until midnight. However, the main problem was that Sam would go to sleep lying on me or his Dad - not in bed.

"We rocked Sam to sleep after his bedtime bottle and put him into his cot already asleep. When he woke naturally, around midnight, he wasn't able to self-soothe and return to sleep without us. This meant we had to rock him to sleep or, in the worst case, bring him into our bed with us.

"Our sleep was disrupted, Sam's sleep was disrupted and we were all worse for it. Controlled crying didn't work; once Sam stood up in his cot and started crying, he would ramp himself up into hysteria very quickly.

"Fi suggested that they key to Sam's sleep difficulty was that we were putting him down for the night already asleep. Sam simply did not know how to get himself back to sleep which was distressing to him - and us!

"Fi suggested that we read a story to Sam and put him in his cot awake but remain close to the cot to soothe him, should he become upset. The first few nights we followed Fi's suggestions and by the time the fourth night rolled around, Sam was asking to go into his bed and happily laid in his cot on his own.

"Some nights Sam will take a while to settle himself but he does so happily, chattering to himself, playing with some of the soft toys in his cot. Occasionally he will call out for us but my husband will go to him, tell him "sleepy time Sammy" and gently settle him back down.

"Not every night is perfect but most nights, Sam is sleeping through and is waking happy and refreshed, as are his Mummy and Daddy.

"Controlled crying was definitely not an option for me, nor for Sam, but I also knew that Fi would never suggest something as dramatic as "cry it out".

"Fi was very conscious of the fact that when Sam starts crying, no amount of ignoring or shushing will bring him back down. Fi gave us a method that was sensitive to Sam's needs.

"I think the fact that Fi believes that each child and family is different is the key to her success with sleep issues. She takes the time to find out exactly what is going on in each family and then, based on the child and their surroundings, is able to offer suggestions that make the transition to good sleep as painless as possible. Fi takes that time and understands that each family needs a tailored approach

"When we buckled down and used Fi's suggestions to help Sam self-settle and self-soothe, we expected to be in for the long haul.

"A few nights was all it took.

"Sam was manipulating us and when Mark and I took a joint stance, singing from the same hymn-sheet, we were able to help our son settle into a positive sleep pattern with very little trauma on either part."

William's story

Ishta is a mum of five. She came to me for help when her fourth child, William, wasn't sleeping.

"I came to Fi when William was nine months old. He wasn't sleeping for more than an hour at a time, wanted feeding every time he woke, and I was a total mess! I was just so tired.

"I guess I didn't really know what to expect from Fi. I'd heard all about controlled crying but I'd never used it and was really open to any advice. I was surprised how quickly Fi's advice helped.

"She tailor-made us a routine which fitted in with our family. It was based on her 'Fi's four for happiness' concept but tweaked to fit around our lives.

"I believe every baby or child is different. But so are parents, which means that as well as fitting the child's routine around their own and those of other family members, they need to be happy. I believe happy parents make happy babies!

"I was amazed how quickly Fi's advice worked! The daytime routine Fi devised seemed to set William up perfectly for bedtime. The first night we tried it was the first night he had gone down in his cot by himself. Within three nights he was sleeping through –

ten hours a night!

"Fi just seems to have this amazing ability to know just what is needed – it seems totally instinctive! I still can't believe that, by email, she was able to create a routine for us around three school runs and three older siblings! The advice was just so easy to read through and follow – it just made sense.

"If I had any advice to parents it would be to seek advice sooner than later. I wish I had!"

Oscar's story

Dawn Brown is a Mum of two. She came to me when her son Oscar, who had health problems, was keeping the whole house awake at night.

"Fi helped us when Oscar was approximately two years and three months old. We had been battling with bedtime for too long and everybody in the house was tired and miserable.

"Due to health problems when he was younger, we had never established a proper bedtime routine and we had got ourselves into a situation where bedtime was taking hours and becoming upsetting for everybody in the family.

"Fi is most definitely how a parenting expert should be. She believes that each child and parent is different. Oscar was our second child and our first child, Zara, was a perfect sleeper from an early age. It wasn't what we were doing that was wrong, it was that Oscar was a different child and needed different things to Zara in order to get to sleep.

"Fi took a lot of time to understand Oscar's health problems and how they would be effecting his bedtime and sleeping routine and to come up with ideas on how we could work around them.

"Fi's advice didn't offer a quick fix, but we had over two years of bad habits to get out of. We knew it was going to be a slow journey to get things back on track.

"Within a couple of months we had reached a much better situation. Six months later bedtime is now a pleasure - the children both clean their teeth and they go and get into bed by themselves.

"I then pop in for a goodnight kiss and cuddle and leave the room. Nine times out of ten Oscar will sleep through the night, although we have still have the occasional bad night due to his health.

"To any parents looking for help with sleep, I'd say don't get despondent if you don't seem to get a quick fix. Sometimes it takes a while for everybody to adjust to new routines, but with patience and determination you will get there eventually.

"Fi has been a godsend to us. We really were at our wits end and the change in all our lives since we finally cracked sleep has been huge.

"Rather than reeling off usual methods, and trust me I have read every book going on the subject, Fi really took time to look at our situation and make us understand Oscar and what he needed to go to sleep. It all makes complete sense to us now but it took somebody from outside the situation to help guide us through the process and make us realise what was really needed."

Gentle but practical

The one thing that has stuck in my mind from helping hundreds of parents each week, is how many parents say they like my gentle but practical approach to parenting.

There's no hard fast rules and regulations and no scary solutions, just practical, sound advice to help others achieve what I have over the years – a happy baby bedtime.

I hope that by following the guides in this book, you will also be able to say goodnight to sleepless nights!

> **Every child is different! You can't have a one-size-fits-all approach to parenting, what works for one family, might not work for another. #everychildisdifferent**

CHAPTER 1

ROUTINE IS THE MAGIC KEY!

Of all the questions I get from parents, 'how can I get my baby into a routine?' seems to be the most frequent. And while routine really is, in my opinion, the magic key to a happy bedtime baby, in those precious early days it's all about settling in.

It's so important that yours and your baby's first weeks are about adapting to your new role as a parent and just enjoying the new life you are starting. Those days hit you in a way you can't really prepare for. The common, and often unsolicited, advice you receive from other parents, telling you to 'enjoy your sleep now because soon it will be gone forever' is just the first piece in a long line of unhelpful pieces of advice about parenting you are likely to be given.

It takes time to adapt to your new role. Your new life. And so I say to parents that the only routine you need to establish in those precious early days is a good feeding pattern. But more on that later.

Becoming a parent can take some getting used to. Nothing could have prepared me for that heart explosion I experienced when I came face to face with Betsy, my first born.

Weighing just six pounds and six ounces, she seemed too tiny to be real. And, after three years of trying and failing to have her, the moment was finally here. I was blown away and totally dumbstruck.

I was a parent.

This tiny thing was ours to care for.

Forever.

Boom!

It was terrifying even for me, as a qualified nursery nurse, so goodness knows how terrified other parents must feel!

When my second child Oscar, was born, less than a year later

(I know! Crazy right?) I was still getting used to being a parent. Yes of course I'd worked with children and newborns for over twenty years, but parenting is whole different ball game to nannying or nursery nursing. It really is!

What I'm trying to say is, please don't worry about routine in those first precious hours, days or even weeks with your baby. Enjoy every second of every day. Cuddle a lot. Sleep a lot. Eat cake a lot, and please, please don't worry about housework. Those days go by so fast and they are so very precious. If I could go back to those days now, I'd do less cleaning, more sleeping, less worrying, and just be so much more relaxed.

Fi's Four for Happiness – The baby routine

I'm pretty chuffed to be able say that in all of my years of working with little ones and their parents I've never had a complaint that my 'Four for happiness' routine hasn't worked. And it has been used by parents across the world - from New York to New Zealand.

I've helped thousands of parents establish a routine by following a simple, gentle guide developed during my professional career as a nanny and then as a mum to two little ones born very close together.

My many years working as a professional nanny were invaluable. I learned that, even with all of my training and qualifications, all babies and parents are different, and that what worked for one, just won't work with another. But one thing really stuck out; routine was the magic key to a good night's sleep.

I noticed that the closer to a four hourly feeding routine babies got, the better they were at sleeping through the night. More of that later for now - it's the basis of my Four for Happiness theory.

Whether you decide to breastfeed or formula feed your baby, there are two methods to choose the frequency of feeds. These methods are demand feeding and routine feeding.

Feeding on Demand:

- Your baby is fed little and often or when they cry out for a feed
- In practice this means your baby does not wait for a feed and is fed 'on demand'

Feeding on a Routine

- Your baby is fed at pre-defined feeding times, set in place throughout the day
- So in practice this will mean your baby will expect to wait to feed at scheduled times and find comfort in other ways until that scheduled feeding time

It is important to say here that it is you, and only you, who can decide what is best for you and your baby. You will receive advice from midwives, parenting advisors and other parents, but ultimately it is you that knows your baby and what is best for them.

I'm very much a 'live and let live' parent and professional. I don't judge others on their parenting methods. I wouldn't like to be judged by my own. I'm not a fan of naming parenting methods (there are too many to list) and I dislike intolerance of others

I have been known to regularly stand up for the formula feeding parent who has been brow beaten by a hardy midwife, but equally I have stood up for the breastfeeding mother who has been asked to leave a cafe for feeding her child in a public place. I believe parenting is about making informed choices, and this book is aimed at giving you the information to make that choice when it comes to your very own happy baby bedtime.

My experiences, both as a mother and a professional, have taught me that babies thrive on routine. That routine could be founded on a two hourly or four hourly feeding pattern but the key thing is the routine be clear and that you stick to it.

Some babies naturally fall into a four hour routine (my two did) and some will want to snack every now and then and have a bigger feed every few hours. You will figure out the best pattern for you and your baby and you will be able to tell whether it's working.

However, one thing you should consider when deciding how often to feed and whether to opt for demand or routine based feeding is that, when you are a new parent it takes a while to learn the difference between your baby's cries.

This is one of the reasons that feeding on demand can go wrong. Feeding your baby every time they cry, rather than soothing them or helping with their trapped wind, for instance, or finding out why they are unsettled for another reason can cause problems for both of you. You will be stressed because they won't feed and they won't feed because they are windy and you end up with tears all round.

In comparison, routine based feeding can be much more helpful and easier for both baby and parent.

Fi's Four for Happiness routine is aimed at parents wanting to follow a feeding routine, not babies fed on demand. However - it can be adapted to suit your needs. You can follow other parts of the schedule with a demand fed baby, (for instance the bath time, play and bedtime parts) but it'll take a little longer to say goodnight to your sleepless nights.

Why? Because throughout the book there are tips and guidelines intended to help your baby self-settle. If you are feeding your baby every time he or she cries, realistically you won't be able to follow the guide properly. Therefore the methods won't work as quickly. They will work eventually. But it'll take longer to see the differences.

Let me tell you my own experiences – as I think you'll relate more to me as a parent than a professional. Yes, I'm qualified, yes I'm experienced, but above all, like you, I'm a parent.

As a mum to two children, born only 364 days apart, it was

essential we followed a routine from birth, especially in the case of my son; Oscar. Coping with a twelve month old and a newborn is no easy task let me tell you – even for a qualified nursery nurse - so routine saved me. It saved us as a family really. I'm sure, no, I know, I'd have pretty much nose-dived into nappy brain state without a routine. My husband looks back on those early days and often says he can't believe how I coped. But I did. Because of routine. (And cake. A lot of cake!)

Sadly many parents are afraid to start a routine. They are worried that their little one won't adapt. Many worry it'll be too difficult, so they stick to their plan of feeding and sleeping on demand. They do this day and night, until months, even years have passed and they have a three year old non-sleeper who demands milk in the small hours.

(Of course – if a parent wants to dream feed their three year old in the night then that is their choice, but I doubt you would have bought this book if that's what you still wanted to do, right?)

A succession of sleepless nights and exhausting days are enough to give any parent a headache. Parenting should be fun, rewarding and enjoyable but on very little sleep it becomes difficult to enjoy sometimes.

As I've mentioned, when you are pregnant, other parents take great delight in telling you about sleep deprivation. They pass on story after story about the zombie state they endure daily, or the amount of sleep they survive on. But it really doesn't have to be like that.

Because of my ability to get children to sleep, I've been called magical in my time. But the rumour hasn't always worked in my favour. On occasion, it has resulted in brand new parents expecting miracles from their brand new baby - and from me!

I have to break it to you – I'm not magical, and it's unlikely your newborn will sleep through the night. Actually, it's highly unlikely.

You see, during the first few months of your little one's life, he or she will want, and need, to sleep deeply and happily in 3-4 hour blocks. Your lovely little newborn will not be awake all day and sleep all night like an adult or older child.

I'm sorry but they are not born to behave that way.

But they can learn to differentiate between night and day. With your help. But more on that later.

So, I'm going to break it to you gently (sorry – as gently as I can), don't expect a full twelve hours sleep for a good few weeks, possibly months.

Please don't worry though, it's only a short time. Focus on this time only being a few weeks and it'll help you keep those heavy eyes open at two in the morning. Focus on the bonding instead - I for one loved the early hours; cuddling and bonding with my newborn babies. Focus on the magic of those early days. They grow so quickly and I promise you, even when you feel totally drained you will look back on this time with fondness.

However, by following my baby bedtime guide, by the time your baby is six weeks old, you will be starting a bedtime routine and then sleep will start to be better.

Of course, sleep is very precious. I've had many sleepless nights caused by illness (I'll cover that later in the book) and I'm not a happy bunny without my eight hours! Just ask my husband – I'm a certified grumpy pants without sleep.

So to help you with those early weeks I'm going to share some things that have helped new parents who came to me for help, and helped me survive those early parenting days with little sleep. These tips are also invaluable when your children are losing sleep, and causing you to miss out as well, because they are poorly.

Top tips for coping with little sleep in the early days!

Shower power! I am not a morning person. My littlies sleep for between 12 and 14 hours most nights so I get a happy bedtime baby sleep every night. And yet I am still not a morning person. The one thing (apart from coffee!) that sorts me out is a hot shower.

It's so very tempting to hang out in your PJs all day and not have a wash in those early weeks. And, while I totally love a PJ day, I have to say a shower will make you feel so much better about facing the day ahead.

I find a nice smelling shower gel works magic! A zesty smelling one gets those senses going and wakes me up. I sometimes even manage a smile before 7.30am!

Joking aside, looking after yourself really helps you to look after your little one, and this morning boost is a great way of helping you to do both.

Coffee and cake: I'm going against the advice of every healthy eating guide every published here, but enjoying a good cup of coffee and a generous slice of cake when things get tough really helps keep tiredness at bay.

I'm not suggesting caffeine overdrive here, just a little happy perk-me-up to keep you going through the day.

However, if you are breastfeeding, and want to avoid caffeine, even just smelling coffee can give you a boost. In *experiments with exhausted laboratory rats, Han-Seok Seo found that coffee aroma helps reduce the stress of sleep deprivation. Clever eh? So sniff those coffee beans my lovelies for that wide-awake feeling.

Of course, if coffee and cake isn't your treat of choice, choose something else uplifting. It's about feeling better; feeling brighter when you are totally and utterly exhausted. And remember – these exhausting days won't last forever.

Healthy eating and energy boosting foods: The last thing you feel like doing when you are exhausted is eating a healthy breakfast; believe me. But did you know eating an hour after waking (on what little sleep you have had) will make you feel more alert and ready for the day ahead? I'm serious! Eating a breakfast that contains slow energy releasing carbohydrates (think porridge with raisins for an extra sugar boost) will soon have you feeling more human.

On my sleep-deprived days (I still get them when the littlies are poorly or have nightmares) I find eating well makes things a little easier. I've listed some of the better exhausted-help-me-now foods below.

Sweet potato: Sweet potato is high in carbohydrates and loaded with vitamin A and vitamin C – and so these little power veggies will help fight off midday fatigue. Perfect for a tired parent lunch! Try slicing into mini fries and roasting in the oven. Then dip in a little hummus for an amazing energy boosting lunch.

Honey: Did you know that a spoonful of honey is nature's equivalent of an energy drink? Smart eh? Not only is it a slow time release energy food, it's also great for a sweet kick instead of sugar. Add to yogurt or add a few drops to your afternoon cuppa for a little boost.

Bananas: Well know as a healthy treat, bananas are an easy snack to carry around with you in your bag! Great for a mid-morning break or to slice and pop on your breakfast! Ha! Who's sleepy now?

Almonds: These magical energy snacks are packed with protein, manganese, copper and riboflavin! Copper and manganese play an essential role in keeping energy flowing throughout the body and Riboflavin aids oxygen-based energy production. What clever little nuts!

Bad night booster!

This fatigue fighting Banana smoothy is both nutritious and delicious and filled with energy boosting ingredients and will give you that little kick you need after an awful night! It's also quite a cold bug fighting remedy too, so great for when you are feeling under the weather!

> **Ingredients:** (makes two smoothies)
> 2 x Bananas
> 2 x tsp honey
> 2 x tsp cinnamon powder
> 2 x pint semi-skimmed milk

Have a power nap! Sounds amazing right? You want in? Ah - but you have a million and one things to do? Forget those things!

Please listen to me. Sleep.

Sleep!

Catch up on sleep when you can in the early days with your baby – it's so important!

I wish I'd not played super-mum in those early days and that I'd napped when my babies did – especially when Oscar was a newborn and Betsy was twelve months old. I was exhausted but still did all those household chores and caught up on my parenting emails.

Don't do as I did - seriously – you'll thank me for it. Sure the house will be a mess, but people will understand! You've had a baby. You're shattered. Sleep. Even if you only get a quick 30 minute catnap, it'll make such a difference to your mind and your body.

> **If you've had a bad night – grab a power nap when your little one sleeps. Even half an hour can make you feel lots better! #powernapthatbadnightaway**

Get some fresh air: Fresh air is just the best remedy for super-shattered parents I promise!

Going out for a walk with your newborn is probably the last thing you feel like doing when exhausted, but it's seriously good for you and your baby! We have a little dog, so for me a daily walk is already part of my routine. A good double buggy meant that, in those early days, my daily walk was easy and I felt so much better for getting out there, away from the house. It woke me up and made me feel so much better.

Now the littlies are older, if we've had a disturbed night due to night terrors or illness, that walk really helps me to get motivated for our day. We pop our wellies on, head out with the dog, and I feel instantly better.

Socialise! I'm not talking a quick half down the local, I'm thinking getting together with fellow parents for a cuppa. If you've made friends at your local baby group or during your pregnancy get together with them during the rubbish no-sleep days. It's great to chat about the bad night-times. It's incredibly therapeutic and you'll most likely find they are going through the same thing too. (If they are, suggest this book!) Add coffee and cake and you're onto a sleep deprivation winner!

Get an early night: I'm not suggesting romancing here – I'm talking super-sleep! Even going to bed half an hour earlier each night will help you to feel better. Don't think of it as catching up on sleep, you'll drive yourself crazy with that thought. (I'm only four years in as a parent and haven't caught up yet on the teething and poorly nights.) Think it as a 'feeling better' solution.

Routine - the magic key

Now we've covered sleep deprivation – let's get back to avoiding it! Let's get back to routines! One question I'm often asked by new and prospective parents is , 'How soon can I start the Fi's four for happiness routine?'

I always advise that you start a routine as soon as you can, but it's not essential. As I've mentioned before, it is far more important in those early days to adapt, cuddle, and just be with your baby. Having said that you can gently start a routine from birth.

By gently, I mean starting with feeding in a routine. Shock, horror! I can hear the gasps already. Some other professionals will possibly disagree with this advice, but as with lots of childcare advice and ideas there is always a difference of opinion. I've yet to find a baby who followed my routine from birth, that doesn't eat, sleep and thrive enormously well. They are happy, developing well, and, my oh my, they are happy bedtime babies!

My own children were in a four hourly feed routine from birth. They were both breast fed, and then combination fed (bottle/ breast/bottle) and by six weeks old they slept through the night from 6pm to 6am. Of course, this included a dream feed at 10pm and sometimes at 2am.

For those who don't already know, the phrase 'dream feed' refers to a feed, either breast or bottle, during which the child doesn't wake. The parent has to be awake though I'm afraid!

Of course we did have a few sleepless nights caused by silent reflux, which I will cover in my chapter on reflux. But this eased as our little ones' oesophagus's matured. In general, my two children, and all of the children whose parents I have advised, are happy sleepers.

A four hour feeding routine works. It's safe (in accordance with NHS guidelines, babies should feed up to every four hours) and the little ones thrive. I have to stress here though lovelies, that routine should not be forced. Most babies will naturally fall into a four hour routine. Mine did, and so did many in my care. Routine is the magic key to a happy bedtime baby and a good night's sleep.

Let's get started with routine

When your baby is very small, it's important to let them sleep lots when they want to in the day. Being a newborn is hard work, it's exhausting in fact! That whole labour thing that wore the baby's mother out, it was hard work for the little one as well! And this new life malarkey? Well, it's tricky, there's a lot of adapting and growing to do! And so they need to sleep.

Don't worry! As I've said before, newborns are made to behave this way. Remember - during the first few months of your little one's life, they will want, and need, to sleep deeply and happily in 3-4 hour blocks throughout the 24 hour period. So don't be expecting to say goodnight to a sleepless night from day one.

For me, with two babies so close together, routine meant by five months old my son and daughter, both in a routine from birth, slept from 6pm to 8am every night and never needed to be picked up out of their cribs during the night unless they were poorly.

They also slept for between two and three hours every afternoon until they were three years old. They were, and still are, happy bedtime babies.

At three and four years old they have always slept through the night. Yes, we have had our teething nights or snuffly cold nights where sleep is disrupted, and as they grew older we had nightmare nights where bad dreams disturbed sleep. But throughout the majority of their little lives they have thrived well because they sleep so well. No - they are not some miracle of nature. They are littlies of routine.

'Routine is the magic key to a happy bedtime baby and a good night's sleep.'

Come on – let me hear you chant it! You can even add a air punch if you wish. No? Maybe later. Sorry, I shouldn't make light of an awful non-sleeping situation, but I'm so excited that you are starting a happy baby bedtime routine that I can't help going over the top.

'Routine is the magic key to a happy bedtime baby and a goodnights sleep.' It is – really it is, and once you've established one, you are on your way to saying goodnight to sleepless nights. Pinky promise.

Not convinced? Let me assure you that every parent who has used my parenting advice service, whose little ones didn't sleep through the night, and who have followed my plans and guidance, now have happy bedtime baby sleepers.

What is Four for Happiness?

'Come on then, what is the *Four for Happiness* routine?' I hear you ask (or did you just skip the whole chapter on why it works and dive straight in here?)

My *Four for Happiness* routine works wonders from birth - but can be started at any age with a little dedication!

'Four for Happiness' is based on four hourly feeds from birth. Sounds regimented? No, don't panic! The routine is not forced. The babies I have worked with, and my own, have naturally adapted to those feeding times. It's gentle.

What if my baby won't wait four hours?

Of course if a baby is hungry you don't starve them, but many parents mistakenly feed their babies for comfort and not for food. It's an easy mistake to make. Of course it is. Your baby cries and the first thing you want do is offer the breast or bottle for a feed. What you are really doing is trying to comfort your baby in the way that seems most obvious and natural.

But deep down you know that babies don't need milk to be comforted. They need milk to grow and thrive, but they need you as a parent to comfort them.

You are pretty amazing, you know? You are a wonderful comfort and entertainment system. Your baby loves all of you – not just your ability to feed them, but your hands for stroking and massage, your voice for singing and arms to cuddle.

(You can be the worst singer in the world and yet your baby will love your voice! Just ask my husband!)

You know those funny faces you pull? Your baby will adore them. All of this wonderful, close bonding can be achieved without the need for constant feeding. Feeding is hard, hard work – give yourself, your boobs (if you're a breastfeeding Mum) and your baby a break.

I loved the closeness of breastfeeding and bottle feeding, but I learned quickly that when my babies needed comforting they necessarily didn't bottle or boob. They needed their Mum or Dad.

You don't need to feed your baby to sleep. You don't need to feed your baby every time they cry. You can! Of course you can. But you don't need to. And that my lovelies is the magic key to a happy bedtime baby and a good night's sleep.

Routine is the magic key to a happy bedtime baby and a good night's sleep. Come on – you're getting it now aren't you? I'm going to make it your ear-worm for today!

But I guess you are eager to know what a routine looks like? So let's talk times. Based on hours that can be easily adapted to suit your life, the basic 'Four for Happiness' is: 6-10-2. So that means you should feed at 6am, 10am, 2pm, 6pm,10pm and 2am as follows.

The Four for Happiness routine

6am - Breast/bottle feed: After the feed, wind your baby well. I'd say a good two to three burps is a good wind!

Then settle baby and let them go back to a milk-happy sleep (and you can have a nap as well!)

At this point you can make a choice. You can either get up before the 10am feed to get showered and dressed before your baby wakes, or stay in bed. You could also get up, shower and freshen up and then head back to bed. However, if you are a brand new mum – I'd go for staying in bed. You need recovery time and this means rest.

10am - Breast/bottle feed: After feeding, wind well again, change nappy, wash baby down, dress and get up and ready for the day.

If you've chosen to sleep in until now, go and grab yourself a shower – it'll help you feel better for the day ahead. If you have a moveable crib or baby chair, bring it to the bathroom door with you so you feel better about hearing baby if they need you.

Newborns will usually sleep again after this feed, but as your baby grows this will become the perfect time for getting out and about for a walk, a trip to baby group or a catch up with friends.

I can't stress enough how important it is to get out and about with your little one. Not in the very early days of course, you'll still be finding your feet as a new parent to start with. But as the days turn into weeks, it's important to go out every day if you can. Just got for a change of scenery or to meet other parents or friends. Even if it's just for a coffee and a cake.

> **Gosh, all she goes on about is cake – anyone would think she was cake obsessed! #CakeisHappiness**

Newborns will sleep on and off with very little wakeful time; but you'll find them starting to stir, once they are in their little routine. This will normally happen around half an hour to fifteen minutes before their feed is due.

12pm - Nappy change: You may have already changed your baby by this point of course. It goes without saying that you should always change your baby if they are wet, even if they have super-duper-clever nappies that seem dry. Your baby's skin is very sensitive and nappy rash is something you want to avoid. However, if you haven't already changed them by twelve, it's a good idea to do so now; even if they aren't wet.

2pm - Breast/bottle feed: After this feed, wind and change your baby, and then settle for naps. It's a great idea to get your baby settled into their crib for an afternoon nap, from very early in their life, rather than holding them while they sleep.

This is because, later on, when they are older, they will have an afternoon nap after their lunch. If they nap in their cot from the very beginning, then they'll associate cot with sleep – perfect for evening bedtime, perfect for when you want to put them to bed for an afternoon nap, and rarely causing bedtime problems when older.

Let them sleep.

When they wake from their nap, which would normally be no later than three pm, take them out of their crib or cot and do a nappy change.

Now is a great time to get out and about again – maybe for a walk or to meet up with friends. (More cake? Too much?)

When your baby is older they'll sleep less and less in the afternoon and a more established sleep routine can be set. For more information on this, see my older baby routine later in the book.

When your baby is very tiny, you'll find they will be asleep at around this time. As they get older you can incorporate play during a wakeful period. There's more on playing with your baby in the Happy Bedtime Baby playtime section later.

5pm - Bath: Aim to bath your baby at around 5pm, and put them into pyjamas, ready for their 6pm feed. I've always used a full size bath, filled to a very shallow level for the children I've looked after, rather than buying a baby bath. For children that can't yet support themselves, you should buy a bath support seat. You can also buy eco-friendly bath dividers, so you don't use up too much water.

6pm - Breast/bottle feed: Ensuring your baby has had a good feed before bed is a great routine to get into. What is even more important is that baby has been winded properly. As mentioned before, a good two to three burps is perfect to ensure little one is wind free and not likely to wake in discomfort and have you pacing the floor.

> **Be prepared – little babies can produce almighty burps! Our two have given us many giggles during their baby years with their almighty burps! #HappyBurpDay**

After this feed it's officially little one's bedtime! Very little babies have most likely already been sleeping for most of the day, but it's a really great routine to get into if you pop them to bed after this feed.

Again, it's good to start as you mean to go on. It's a great way of them getting used to the fact that being in their cot means its sleep time. It's the best way to help your baby become a happy bedtime baby and make sleepless nights a very rare occurrence.

It's crucial to remember that, when baby is out of sight, for safety's sake, always use a good baby monitor. There is more on this in the 'Snug as a bug' chapter of the book.

10pm- Breast/bottle feed: It's likely that this will be a dream feed; where your baby is in bed already and is half asleep for their feed. So, he or she will be stirring for a feed, but won't be fully awake. It is best if you feed in the room where they sleep, and avoid putting any bright lights on. Try not to interact as this will stimulate your baby into a more wakeful phase - then settling them back to sleep will be more difficult.

My two rarely woke for this feed and fed quietly and sleepily. I always found that by leaving the landing light on it gave enough light to see what I was doing, but not enough to fully wake them.

After this dream feed, wind your baby well, change their

nappy if necessary and settle them back into bed.

2am - Breast/bottle feed: Again, this is a dream feed. As before, feed in the room where they sleep and again, avoid putting any bright lights on. You'll most likely be half asleep yourself here, so it's important to mention that if you are feeding in bed, don't fall fully asleep yourself, as hard as this may be. I'll go into more detail about safer ways of co-sleeping later in the book.

I must say here, as a Twitter fan, these feeding hours for me were aided by Twitter friends who were also awake feeding their babies! I also have a friend, Dawn, who had a baby the same age as Oscar, and was following my routine guide. We'd text each other while feeding at 2am! It made me smile when I was feeling exhausted and I think it made her smile and helped get us both through those tiring nights! So get yourself a feeding buddy! Honestly – it really helps!

So that's the basic routine – the feedback from parents using the advice service is that it's easy enough to follow. The timings seem to work well with most families, and it fits in with school run times! You won't need to be feeding when you are supposed to be on a school pick up!

Remember though, from birth, in those precious early days, this routine can be a little more relaxed. It's hard enough adapting to parenting without following rigid routines.

It's your baby, your life and your routine.

Tweak the hours to suit your life and your own routine if need be, but try and stick as closely to the four hour plan as you can. Don't stress baby or yourself at 5.30am by refusing to feed until 6am.

Don't panic if it's 9pm and little one wakes, genuinely hungry, and needs milk and it's not yet before 10pm. Go by your baby, just keep the routine in the back of your mind and try and stick to it because (come on, say it with me!) Routine is the magic key to a happy bedtime baby and a good night's sleep.

Cutting the 2am feed

This idea excites you doesn't it? It did me, when mine were little. Whoop, whoop! No more night owl feeds! Really? Yes really.

From around six weeks old, when your baby naturally stops waking for a feed or stirring for a dream feed you can drop it! Sounds too good to be true? No, not really.

Of all the parents who asked me for sleep tips, around 85% of their children had stopped waking for their 2am feed once they had been established in the Fi's Four for Happiness routine. Mine stopped waking for their 2am feed at around six weeks old too.

> **Around 85% of the parents I have shared *Fi's Four for Happiness* with are able to stop the 2am feed at six weeks #NoMoreZombieMum**

Did I love that they stopped waking for that feed? Honestly – I missed it. I missed those early hours being awake with my little baby, when the rest of the world was sleeping. That quiet hush of night. Those snuggles and time that was just us. Those fun tweets and texts with fellow night-owls. BUT – I was so glad to get a full night's sleep. Especially with my second baby.

Having two children so close together was pretty hard going on very little sleep. Having two children so close together after a good night's sleep was much more fun! Saying goodnight to sleepless nights was, for me, pretty great.

You should think of this as a guide though – some babies will stop the early morning dream feed much later. Don't drop this feed until your baby is ready. If they stop waking for the feed and you have to wake them for it, then after a week of doing so, you can stop.

This routine can be followed until weaning begins, which is usually between the age of four and six months, depending on how hungry you find your baby is.

When weaning is established, the times in the routine are changed to fit in with breakfast, lunch and dinner. You'll find the weaning baby routine and guide in the weaning routines chapter. Together with a couple of exciting first recipes for little tummies!

How do I stick to the routine when my baby is unsettled?

It's important to stick to this routine as closely as possible or it won't work. I'm being honest here, feeding every two hours one day and then every four hours the next, then back to three and then to hourly – it's not a routine. It's not going to ever become a routine. And, sadly, it's not going to help you say goodnight to sleepless nights.

Feeding on demand is something many parents want to do in the very early days. In fact, some professionals recommend feeding on demand if is something you want to do for your own sake. Most recommend you return to routine when it comes to the crunch though.

Try to avoid feeding your baby in-between the routine hours as this will cause confusion and is essentially, feeding on demand by another name.

If your baby is unsettled, you can try using a dummy, as often babies don't want the milk but rather the comfort of sucking. Dummies, pacifiers, doo-doo's, suckies, tut-tuts (yes, people call them all kinds of things) are great ways of comforting little ones and often help with conditions such as silent reflux.

My two loved comfort sucking. Betsy had a dummy from a young age and it really helped her reflux. Oscar rejected dummies for his thumb which he still sucks - he's three now and there's no getting that thumb away! However, if you are breastfeeding it's best to wait at least four weeks or until breastfeeding is established before introducing a dummy as it can confuse breastfed babies.

The times when even routine won't help

There are times when routine goes out of the window, when your little one is unusually unsettled and you just have to ride the wide-awake, sleepless night train until everything is back to normal. Those times may include:

When your baby is poorly: It's so important if you suspect your baby is poorly not to follow sleep guides, or any sleep training. I'm sorry to break it to you – but a poorly baby will more than likely result in a sleepless night or two or three. There is lots of advice in the poorly poppet section on helping little ones to feel more comfortable, and tips on coping with sleepless nights.

When your baby is really hungry: Remember, as your baby grows they will become hungrier and have growth spurts. The sleepy newborn, may suddenly develop a super-duper appetite.

If you find your baby is hungrier in between the four hour routine, you may need to increase the size of feed at one of the *Four for Happiness* time slots. If you are breastfeeding you'll most likely find your milk naturally accommodates your baby's hunger. If your baby is formula fed, you'll need to check the guide for age, and increase accordingly. If your baby is approaching the weaning months, a hungry baby may be a sign that you should start introducing solid food.

When your baby is teething: Teething sucks. I'm sorry – but it does, and no amount of experience or qualifications will turn a teething baby into a happy sleeper during the most painful days of teething.

I'm a mum. I've been walking the floor with two babies at one time teething (that took some juggling let me tell you!) Again, this is another of the not-so-fun things about having two babies so close together. However, don't be too alarmed reading this. There are a few tips and ideas in chapter eight, Poorly Poppets, that can make teething a little less rubbish.

Let's play! Encouraging play as part of your baby's routine

Play is a really important part of your little one's routine.

Playing is one of my favourite things about being a parent. Now my two are older, we get to have some fabulous fun, but I didn't have to wait until they were toddlers. I'd urge you to encourage your child to play and take part in playing with your baby from day one.

As I've mentioned before – stimulating your baby during wakeful time is essential for routine and is great for bonding. There is no need for expensive musical soft toys or rattles. You are a great form of entertainment for your baby and you are all they really need in those early months.

Your touch, smell and sound are what your baby needs in-between feeds. Cuddle together, sing songs and read stories. Even from birth babies love to be read to! My husband read *Winnie the Pooh* every night to our little girl, from the day she was born until she was at an age where her demands involved Gruffalo's and princesses!

Happy baby play!

Forget what the baby catalogues suggest and the adverts with bright, shiny toys say. You don't really need to invest in expensive toys, just a few basics and you'll be on your way to happy play!

To ensure a happy baby play time with your baby, here are some ideas that you can incorporate into the daily routine.

1.You! Yes! You are your baby's best toy! You're pretty awesome you know?

Lay your baby down and kneel over them, making funny faces. Stick your tongue out and you might get a shock; they often do it right back at you from a very young age! Make faces, wave your fingers and hands, let them reach up and touch your face. Lay down next to them to encourage them to roll towards you.

Repetition is important – the games you play at first probably won't achieve anything, but play peek-a-boo daily and soon you'll get a response!

Try peek-a-boo with a soft scarf. Put it over your head and then reveal your face and say 'Boo!' Then try it with your baby, gently place the scarf on their face, remove and say boo!

If your baby is smiling, making noises and babbling you are doing well – if they turn away or cry, try something else. You are an entertainment machine! Make some noise or sing! Have fun!

2. Bright fabrics and blankets: Lie your baby near these so they can see clearly. Think crinkly material, cardboard, soft woolly scarves and furry teddy bears. Wave chiffon scarves above baby's head moving them lightly forward and back. Let your little one feel the fabrics, but remember to never leave them unattended with material or scarves that they could choke on.

3. The great outdoors: Get out and about as soon as you can. The fresh air and stimulation promotes a healthy appetite and sleep! It's also great for those exhausting days when you've had a bad night! Make sure baby can see everything. So many parents hide their newborns snugly under hooded prams thinking it keeps them safe and war. It does, but they're missing out on seeing the great big colourful world around them!

4. Black and white images: New Babies love black and white. At this young age, clear bold shapes are fabulous! Print pictures from the internet of big shapes, spots and stars or buy black and white boldly printed soft-play books. Hang black and white striped material nearby to help interest your baby in its surroundings.

5. Swimming! It's never too early to go swimming! Once your baby has had their first jabs they'll be safe to swim.

I took both my little ones swimming at seven weeks old and they love it still. It's always best to go a good, clean pool that has family changing facilities if you can. Also make sure the water is not too cool and don't stay in too long as babies can get cold very quickly. Ensure they are wearing swim nappies to avoid any accidents and, for very young babies, a wet suit can help keep them warm.

If you don't have a local swimming pool, a paddling pool outdoor is great fun in the summer. Fill with warm water, rather than ice cold water from the outside tap, and remember to never leave a baby unattended in or near water.

6. Reading: Reading aloud to your baby is a lovely, bonding activity that you can continue for years to come. Reading aloud teaches your little one about communication and introduces concepts such as numbers, colours and shapes in a fun way. It also helps them to understand the world around them as they grow and turn from babies into toddlers.

Reading books is also a fabulous part of the bedtime routine. I'm a huge fan of books, not only because they are wonderful places to escape to with the little ones (we love our story time adventures) but because hearing your speech helps to build a big catalogue of different words in their brains.

Children who grow up in houses with more than 400 books are proven to get better exam results when they get older. The crazy thing is, it doesn't matter if the child even reads the books or what the books are about, their results still improve!

7. Baby play gyms: A baby gym is a colourful play mat with a built in mobile toy suspended over the top and I love them! You can spend a fortune on a super-duper design, or get a simple design for around £30 and add to it yourself with crinkly material and colourful fabrics.

Play Gyms are fantastic as they help develop hand-eye coordination when babies reach for things and also encourage rolling over while baby is on the floor. Remember to try and have at least ten minutes a day of tummy time to avoid flat head syndrome!

Flat head syndrome, which, as the name suggests entails a flattening out of the back of the head, is a condition that arises as the result of a baby being left in one position for too long.

8. Socialise: Get together with other parents. It's great to get babies used to other children and adults from a young age and great for you too. Check out your local mother and baby groups or other clubs such as Baby Sensory, breastfeeding groups and playgroups. Lots of community centres also hold baby clubs such as singing or get-togethers for local parents.

If playgroups aren't your thing, get together with family or friends for a natter over a cuppa. It's as important for you as it is for baby.

9. Music: My little ones adore music – any music to be fair - and they are not alone in their love of a good tune. Lullabies and nursery rhymes are soothing and engaging for babies and toddlers and music is even good for our little one's health. Premature babies in intensive care units have been found to gain weight faster and leave the hospital sooner when they listen to 30 minutes of Mozart a day. How very clever is that?

Children love any music but babies need something a little softer, so try some classical. Pop it on in the background, and ensure it's not too loud for tiny ear-drums!

10. Singing: Singing with your little baby is a brilliant way to support learning. One of the biggest benefits of singing is the repeated use of the 'memory muscle'. Learning a piece of information attached to a tune, embeds that information more rapidly in a child's mind.

Learn some old fashioned nursery rhymes and sing them to your baby while doing the actions. Baby will follow your hands with their eyes and later will imitate you. Join a singing group, like *Monkey Music* for singing fun with other babies and parents.

Of course, with everyday life it's hard to find the time to fit in lots of activities with your baby, but remember these days fly by. Put the housework on hold and enjoy these early days - the more you put into your baby the more you'll get back! Big wide eyes, bright smiles and gurgles all come from interaction and play. Clapping hands comes from copying and repetition.

The most important thing to do is enjoy your baby and don't worry too much about going overboard on the toy collection.

Massage is another interactive play and bonding idea. This is also a fabulous settling technique that many parents are frightened to try. Enrol yourself in a baby massage class – or find my tutorial on YouTube – it's so easy to do and a really lovely one-to-one session for you and your little one.

Remember this routine has been used by hundreds of parents but it's not everyone's cup of tea. Many health visitors and midwives advise parents that babies should feed on demand and this is simply a matter of opinion. I have to say my own midwife was more than happy with my babies and their routines. After all they were putting on weight, happy, thriving and I was feeling happy.

> **Not every routine can be everybody's cup of tea (or piece of cake)! #Live&LetLive #CakeisHappiness**

Of course, you don't have to follow the *Four for Happiness* routine, it's not right or wrong. I'm just sharing a routine that has worked for over 20 years and has produced healthy, thriving children who eat and sleep well. That's what this book is about – it's sharing the knowledge and experience I have gained as a nursery nurse, nanny and a mum.

As I have said before in this book, you know what is best for your baby. I can advise, show you the way to a happy bedtime baby, but you must always do what you feel is right for you and your baby. It's not a simple case of one size fits all. Something that works for some babies won't work for others. Which is why we'll cover other, more unusual, sleep issues in this book.

Remember routine is the key to a good night's sleep – so get into a regular daily routine if you can - out in the mornings for fresh air and fun, an afternoon nap, and meeting up with other mums too – it's all great for both you and baby!

CHAPTER 2

NIGHT-NIGHT TIME...

I love bedtime. I think as a parent to two very active littlies, I'm pretty tired so when my bedtime comes so I welcome it. I'm so happy that my children welcome bedtime too, and, although on occasions they protest about going to bed (usually if we have visitors and they want to stay up and join the fun), generally they go to bed with smiles. Often ask to go to bed before their actual bedtime!

I know this love of bedtime is down to a great daily routine, an active day and, most importantly, a great bedtime routine.

I can't begin to tell you the importance of a that bedtime routine. Many parents who come to me for sleep advice for their little ones don't have a good bedtime routine. For me it is essential to a good night's sleep. It's especially important for older children – for instance pre-schoolers who need sleep to grow and thrive.

> **Sleep is important for learning and development. It's also great for avoiding the zombie look in parents #RoutineistheMagicKey #ZombieMum**

Did you know that during REM (rapid eye movement) sleep your little ones brain cells are making important connections called synapses. Now without wanting to go too super-sciencey on you, it's actually quite important to know how valuable sleep is.

These synapses enable all learning, movement, and thought. Not only that, research has suggested that too little sleep can effect growth and the immune system, so saying goodnight to sleepless nights benefits everyone!

There are so many easy, simple steps you can take to achieve a perfect bedtime routine, and there are many things you may not be aware of that you should avoid too!

A bedtime routine is a wonderful way to spend time with your little one at the end of a long day. Many parents, when tired, rush it all too quickly, so the magical bonding of the bedtime hour is lost. That glass of wine or favourite TV programme might seem tempting now, but once the children are in bed, or even worse when they are heading off to University, you will regret every rushed moment.

I love the quietness of bedtime with my littlies. The stories, the chat about our day, and before that, when they were babies, the quiet bedtime feed after their bath. The smell of their baby hair and the sound of them feeding before sleep is magical.

There is also magic in putting them into their cot awake and babbling and knowing they were happy. Leaving the room with no tears or noise. Happy bedtime babies.

They are much the same now, only they look at books and happily chat with each other before falling asleep. It's the important routine they are so used to that has given them the gift of a happy bedtime.

I believe, in order to have a happy bedtime baby, it's so important to make bedtime a happy, magical time. A time that little ones enjoy and want to happen, rather than dread and cry and fight about. Starting the bedtime routine unhappy or super wired, isn't going to make bedtime fun for either of you. By following these simple bedtime routine tips, you'll be on your way to a happy bedtime baby for always.

Wind down for bedtime: Spend at least half an hour before the bedtime routine begins winding down from the excitement of the day with a quiet activity. My husband is guilty of breaking this rule often with his game of *Daddy Monster,* which involves him chasing our two up the stairs to the bathroom in a screaming excited pre-bath frenzy, until he is gently reminded that it is actually a time for relaxation and sleep.

Obviously he is glad to see them at the end of the day. But for the children the excitement builds and builds until there's a flurry of tears. So we try and limit the excitement to him returning home with big lovely 'hellos', before winding down for bed.

As lovely as Daddy monsters are, monsters, screaming and bedtime don't go well together. They can also trigger night fears as we found out the hard way with our two. (You can read all about night-time fears and how to deal with them in chapter seven, *Things that go Bump in the Night.*)

A gentle TV program, a story or even colouring for older children are all great ways of getting little ones to sit quietly before going up to bed. For babies, it's a little bit different, but always good to start the bedtime routine as you mean to continue. This is just my idea of a perfect bedtime routine that will ensure a happy bedtime baby child and thus a happy bedtime baby night's sleep.

Bed time routine step one: Bath time

Bath times start the whole bedtime routine with a bang. They really do, so try and get into a daily routine of baths before bed. I know many children suffer with Eczema and so parents are afraid to bath them daily. However, my two have it and I find it actually helps their skin to bath daily, especially without bubble bath or with medically prescribed, skin kind alternatives.

Baths are the best way to start the bedtime routine – not just because babies and little ones create an awful lot of mess and need cleaning often, but because it creates a trigger in the brain. When activated this trigger flicks the bedtime switch that this is the unconscious start of bedtime in your child's minds. It really is the perfect way to start the bedtime routine.

Bath time is also lots of fun. You can buy so many games and toys for the bath, but for very little ones, just the feel of the warmth of the water will help prepare their little bodies for rest. Older ones may like the routine of bath toys and use it as a time to have one last play before bed.

The regularity of bath time will prompt the slow transition from day time to night-time and give you that helping hand in letting them know the night-time routine has begun.

> **By getting into this regular routine, littlies very quickly realise that #Bath=Bed and that it's fun and something to look forward to**

My two know it. They love it. But most importantly of all - they want it! And to me, it's part of a good bedtime routine. When little ones want to go for a bath, even when they know it's the start of bedtime and thus the end of a fun day, you know you are onto a winning bedtime routine.

There are many bath-sleep products out there to buy, such as baby sleep bath, baby sleep body lotions and body wash – but you don't really need them. Especially when your little one is tiny! A basic baby hair and body wash is fine. The warm water itself is enough to relax little ones.

Older children are often happy enough playing with an empty shampoo bottle and plastic cups. All you really need is a warm bath, lots of splashing and playing fun and a warm fluffy towel to dry them off with afterwards.

It is important to say here that you should never leave a child unattended in a bath – not even for a minute and certainly never leave older siblings who are bathing with younger ones in charge of their younger sibling's safety.

Don't leave a child in the bathroom alone if there is water in the bath. And always empty the bath afterwards, ensuring it's fully empty before you leave the bathroom.

Check the water temperature before putting children into the bath. This may sound like common sense but there have been many accidents where parents failed to check the temp and scolded their child's feet putting them in.

You can buy bath thermometers but the easiest way of testing is with the underside of your wrist. Don't use your elbow - especially if you have tough calluses there as it will be less sensitive to temperature.

Bed time routine step two: Baby massage

Massage isn't everyone's cup of tea, but my two, when tiny, adored being massaged. They much prefer a cuddle and a story now, as massages make them roar with laughter, which isn't an advisable thing for bedtime.

However, baby massage is good because:

The power of touch is instinctive: You hold and stroke

and soothe your baby all the time probably without realising it. Baby massage is simply an extension of this and a lovely way of soothing your baby before sleep.

It's a good bonding experience: Massage is a good way for you and your baby to get to know each other and to spend a bit of quality time together.

It's healthy: Studies have suggested that physical contact is good for babies, improving their breathing, circulation, digestion and growth. In fact, baby massage can provide relief for a variety of conditions – massaging your baby's tummy, for example, can help ease reflux, colic, or constipation.

Massaging the gums through the skin can help with the pain of teething and a gentle face massage can help to ease a blocked nose.

It stimulates baby's senses: Massage provides a good source of sensory and muscle stimulation, which is beneficial to all babies, but may be particularly good for babies with special needs.

Regularly massaging your baby will help it to sleep better because it raises levels of the 'feel-good' hormone antitoxin in both you and your baby, helping you both feel calmer and relaxed.

Bed time routine step three: Dressing for bed

After a massage, or bath, dress your baby for bed. With older ones, letting them dress themselves is a great way of encouraging independence. Let them choose their own pyjamas – it's fun and less chaotic at night (and to be honest, it doesn't matter what combination they choose at bedtime because nobody sees).

Remember, with babies in particular, not to overdress - depending on the weather. Think about how comfortable they will be and also think about their bedding and dress them accordingly. It is so important to stress here that babies can overheat very quickly. This can make them uncomfortable and may, in very extreme cases, result in febrile convulsions.

If you are using a baby sleeping bag, then avoid a vest and pyjamas and just opt for pyjamas. The same goes for older children. Don't over dress, and avoid uncomfortable night-wear. Princess nighties (the ones with long skirts) are very pretty but they also are uncomfortable and not really suitable bed wear The same goes for the recent super trendy, super-hero PJs. Ditch that cape before bedtime Batman!

Think safe. Think comfy

Always use a good nappy at bedtime as wetting can cause terrible discomfort and, in turn, cause night-time waking.

There are many great brands that make super-duper nappies for bedtime. It's worth investing in good ones for night-time at least, even if you use slightly cheaper brands at other times. If you use cloth nappies in the day, it may be worth investing in a few disposables for night time comfort and dryness.

Make sure your little one's nappy is fitting properly – a too tight nappy can cause wind and tummy problems which in turn causes a sleepless night.

Brush those teeth!

As your baby grows and teeth pop up, incorporate teeth brushing into your bedtime routine.

Use a soft bristle baby toothbrush with a tiny smear of fluoride toothpaste. Don't worry if you don't manage to brush much at first. The important thing is to get your baby used to teeth-brushing as part of their daily routine.

Bed time routine step four: Read a story

Books are magical. By encouraging a love of books from a young age you are giving your baby the key to their own imagination. Babies that are used to a bedtime story, become children that read to themselves in bed.

Whether your child adores an adventure story before sleep or feels like a fairy tale before bed, it's essential to have a good supply of books to hand. You don't need to spend a fortune either – there are lots of second hand shops and online seconds stores to buy books from. And car boots often turn up wonderfully cheap books. Don't forget your local library as well. While borrowing books isn't ideal for very little ones, simply because they like to repeat the same stories over and over again for months on end, library sales are a great place to buy books. And if it teaches your little one to love the inside of a library when they get older, so much the better.

Even tiny babies loves stories - the sound of your voice is calming, and it really doesn't matter which book you choose when they are very small, because they are listening to the lulling tone of your speech rather than your words.

It's important to mention here with older children, to try and avoid scary stories which could induce nightmares or night terrors (something I'll cover later in the book in chapter seven).

My favourite stories are the old classics like *Winnie the Pooh, Peter Rabbit* and wonderful magical tails of fairies and adventure such as *Peter Pan*. Happy bedtime stories make for happy sleepers.

> **It doesn't really matter what you read to your child when they are too young to understand, but it's probably best to avoid the scary bits from Harry Potter until they are a bit older! #BooksMakeBedtimeHappy**

It's important to point out at this point that, although those soppy movies where the parent reads a child to sleep may look cute, it's not a great habit to get into. I'll explain why...

You should let them fall asleep themselves. It's so important to put your baby to bed half asleep rather than fully asleep, so they can learn to settle themselves. This is really, really important as they grow older and experience the wakeful sleep phase, which we all do, before gently falling back to sleep. If they can only fall asleep while you are reading to them (or cuddling them for that matter) they will not be able to re-settle when this happens.

This is one of the most common problems when it comes to early-wakers or non-settlers. The inability to settle during those moments creates hours of sleepless nights for parents and child.

The same goes for singing or rocking your little one to sleep – as tempting and beautiful as it is. (I'll admit to having done far more times than I should have.) You really are creating a routine that you'll have to keep up. Imagine doing it when your baby isn't so little, isn't so easily settled, isn't so light in your arms. For instance when they are three years old and will only go to sleep this way, because it's the only way they know. Not such a movie time dreamy thought now, eh?

By helping your baby to fall asleep without the need for a crutch such as singing, swaying, stroking or rocking, you'll be giving your baby the best start and encouraging them to become an independent happy sleeper.

Of course this routine is just a guide, but it's one that truly works and has solved many non-sleep cases and created countless happy bedtime babies. By following this routine every night, the parents who came to me with non-settlers, and early wakers, now have happy bedtime baby sleepers.

Their babies and little ones have now become confident in going to bed and settling themselves.

CHAPTER 3

HAPPY NAP-TIME = HAPPY NIGHT-TIME

It surprises me how many parents get in touch with me about their unhappy sleepers and tell me they don't let them nap in the day in case it stops them sleeping at night.

Naps in the day are so important – they help your little one have a good night's sleep. But why? Lots of parents say it doesn't seem logical.

Well, overtired babies and toddlers often have trouble sleeping! If they are overtired at bedtime they will find it harder to settle and often get into such a state they become distressed and wired!

There's no hard rule for napping, but as a guide an hour to three hours each day is good.

Babies under twelve months should have half an hour to an hour in the morning and an hour to three hours in the afternoon. Toddlers aged one to three should have from an hour to two hours in the afternoon.

As my 'older baby' routine suggests - naps should not be taken late in the afternoons, and little ones should be awake by 3.30 or 4.00pm at the latest, to ensure they are ready for their 'big' sleep at bedtime.

Naps are best taken in the night time bed – so for babies their cot or crib, and for toddlers their bed.

Of course this isn't always easy for busy parents, and many find their little ones napping in the buggy or car! As a rule try and keep the majority of their naps in their beds.

Why?

Because associating sleep in the day with their night-time bed makes for better settling at night. They associate the end with sleep and self-settling is so much easier to achieve. I'll be covering self-settling more in the next chapter.

> **Always let children nap in their night time bed #TopSleepTips**

CHAPTER 4

ROCK-A-BYE - KISS SLEEP GOODBYE

Rocking a tiny baby to sleep is truly wonderful, hey – rocking any baby to sleep is pretty special, but it won't help them to learn to settle themselves.

It's a really bad habit to get into, as lovely as it seems at the time. Believe me, I've been on the breaking-this-habit end of the equation many times in my career and I can tell your that rock-a-bye means kiss sleep goodbye.

I have many parents who have come to me for help because their three year old still needs to be rocked to sleep. Now I bet these parents don't have bingo wings like non-rockers such as yours truly, but they are not getting the sleep they and their little ones need and deserve. Why? Because their little ones can't self-settle. They haven't learned this gift of settling themselves back to sleep.

I'm not talking singing themselves a lullaby. It's just the process of learning that, when it's still night-time and the child stirs or begins to wake, perhaps startled by a noise or just feeling uncomfortable, they can allow themselves to drift back to sleep without any external stimulus.

Babies and children who have always been rocked to sleep and not left (happily) to drift off to sleep, need help to get back to sleep. That help is you. Rocking. Back and forth on little sleep, arms aching. You go to put them down, thinking they are asleep and, oh no! They are awake again.

And repeat.

And repeat.

And my arms are falling off! Sound familiar?

You need to let your baby have the opportunity to learn to self-settle. Let me put it another way - imagine your baby is at the age where they should be starting to crawl, but they can't because you are always holding them. So then they never have the opportunity to figure it out, they never learn to crawl and never learn to walk. It's the same with self settling - they have to learn to go to sleep.

Remember - if you always rock your baby to sleep, they will never learn to self settle.

You can teach your baby how to self settle using gentle techniques. There really is no need to use controlled crying unless you really want to and are very confident.

> **There are lots of ways to teach your baby to self settle, controlled crying is my least favourite but some parents like to use this method #Live&LetLive**

In all honesty I have used controlled crying in the past during my career and it works if used correctly. But it's my least favourite method of helping little ones to self-settle. And in my opinion, if you can help your baby settle without tears – that's far nicer isn't it?

Controlled crying has had a bad press in the past few years due to parents not following the controlled crying guide correctly and leaving babies to cry for long periods of time.

Controlled crying is a method that involves leaving your baby to cry for short periods of time, going back to check they are OK, and repeating. There are more details on controlled crying later in this book because, although I don't necessarily recommend it for everyone, I wanted to include a safe way of doing it - rather than ignoring the idea parents use it altogether.

My preferred method, and a much gentler way is my *shh-shh-pat-pat* technique.

The *shh-shh-pat-pat* technique

Pop your baby in their crib or cot and stand nearby. (If it's an older child, do the same by their bed.) If they start to whimper, simply say Shh-Shh very gently. Don't pick them up. It's so important not to pick them up because they need to learn to self settle.

They are not crying just stirring. It's a new thing for them to be put into a cot awake – they are figuring it all out!

If they begin to cry, simply lean over and say Shh-Shh and at the same time gently pat their tummy. You can stroke if you prefer, but remember – you're not doing this to get them to sleep, just to calm them.

Now move away from the cot and wait. If they stir but don't

cry, leave them. If they cry, repeat the shh-shh-pat-pat technique.

Don't use any words. It's especially important with older babies not to enter into a conversation. Just ignore and repeat - Shh-shh-pat-pat and try to avoid eye contact, they don't need the stimuli, they need to go to sleep. This means limited interaction with you.

Keep repeating until they are almost asleep. The important thing is to not pat them to sleep because then you are just replacing rocking with patting. You'll not thank me for a creaky back from nights of patting them to sleep over their cot!

Use this method if they wake in the night. Don't lift them unless they are seriously distressed, wet, soiled or poorly. It's natural of course to want to do that, but in the early days of teaching self settling, it's important to help them to settle themselves.

The bed bottom-shuffle!

Don't laugh! The bed bottom shuffle is what it is; bottom shuffling! This is one of the favourite techniques that I recommend among the parents who come to me for help. It's an even more gentle way and, although it takes much longer to achieve a full night's sleep, it works well. It works with babies in cots and older children in beds too – so it's also one of my favourite techniques.

Now, many parents don't like either the controlled crying or *Shh-Shh-Pat-Pat* techniques and that is fine. As I have said all the way through this book, it is your baby; you know your baby and know what will work for them and you best.

> **It might not be glamorous, but it's gentle and it works #TheBottomShuffle is a great alternative to controlled crying**

The bottom shuffle is a lovely, calm way of sleep training a baby, but it takes longer to say goodnight to a sleepless night.

One of the parents that has used my advice service, Karin who is featured in the introduction to this book, wasn't keen on controlled crying or the *shh-shh-pat-pat* technique. So I suggested the bottom shuffle which, with time, dedication and effort, ensured her little boy was able to sleep through the night and self settle again.

If you want to try the technique as well, sit by your little one's cot when he or she is crying and calmly say, 'shh' and hold their hand. Stroke their arm or head or pat them.

The idea of this is pretty much the same as the *Shh-Shh-Pat-*

Pat technique, but you're you stay with your baby until they fall asleep. As before, you must try and avoid stroking them to sleep, but instead just 'be there' if you can.

The majority of parents who use this technique tell me their babies learn to self settle in less than 10 days. They weren't stroked to sleep. They simply fell asleep knowing their parent was beside them.

As the days move on, you can move further and further away from the cot until you are near the door. Your baby will still be able to see you at this point. It is surprising, in my own experiences and those of others, how quickly this works.

Eventually you move outside the door still saying, 'shh-shh'. You will find there is no need to stay in the room.

It's a very long-winded self-settling technique but it works.

It sounds simple but it can take days to go from holding hands, to letting go and sitting nearby. It works. But it takes lots of time, patience and dedication.

If your baby wakes in the night, repeat the technique - unless they are poorly, soiled, wet or otherwise upset in which case you should care for them as normal.

CHAPTER 5

MULTIPLE HAPPY BABY BEDTIMES

Becoming a parent for the first time is very exciting, but can also be quite worrying. Becoming a parent of twins or triplets can be even more daunting. So I've written this chapter for multiple parents everywhere in the hope that it'll make things a little less scary!

Double trouble? It doesn't have to be…

Looking after one newborn can be hard enough, but when you need to split your time between two or more, it's easy to become overwhelmed. You may even find yourself feeling exhausted unless you handle everything well.

But don't panic - happy multiple sleepers is possible!

For happy baby bedtimes, and to say goodnight to sleepless nights, I'm a firm believer that routine is the key. Now, I'm not talking about a regimented, sticking rigidly to the hour kind of routine, just a gentle and easy routine that fits in with your life.

Routine is the magic key to happy baby bedtimes…

When I talk about routine, I mean feeding, bedtime, naptimes and regular daily activities. Even from a very young age your babies will thrive on routine, such as a regular morning outing to the park or a meeting other parents. Regular feeding times and regular nap and bedtimes are the key to happy baby bedtimes.

If your little ones have been in neonatal care, which many multiple birth babies often are, they are likely to be in a routine created by the care team already. It's a really good idea to stick to this routine.

Change an already established and working feeding routine isn't advisable and can cause chaos – especially if you are dealing with more than one child. So stick to the times for feeding as best you can. Simply adapt it as they grow older and their needs change.

A multiple feeding routine…

However you decide to feed your children, a gentle feeding routine is essential for multiple babies. Feeding multiple babies on demand can leave you feeling exhausted and feeding constantly of course. It's fair to say not a lot else will get done!

That said, it is possible to breastfeed twins and, in some cases, triplets. Breast milk has fantastic benefits for all little ones, but it's important to mention that it's especially helpful for premature babies as their tummy is immature and breast milk is easier to digest.

But please don't worry if you're formula feeding – as with all things parenting it's about making informed choices, so please don't feel guilty if you can't breastfeed.

Sometimes it may be necessary, in the case of multiple births, to use a combination of breastfeeding and formula feeding. Whatever you decide a gentle routine will help. You may also decide to express some breast milk and feed using bottles sometimes so you can share the feeding routine with your partner or family in the early days; at least until you become a super multiple feeder! It's good to get a little family help if you can and ease off the feeding tiredness that parenting multiple birth babies brings!

If your little ones are not in a routine already, and they haven't started life in neonatal care picking up a routine in the process, then aim for a three to four hour feeding schedule. it will be closer to three hours in those early days, moving closer to four as they establish a good feeding pattern and get into a routine.

As soon as you can, try and get your little ones to distinguish daytime from night-time. You can do this by being quieter around naps and bedtime, using your wind down, quietening activities and stories as discussed earlier. You can also try and be a little louder when they are awake, by doing the mundane household chores like vacuuming. Alternatively, put some music on and keep the children entertained whilst teaching the difference between day and night!

Babies are very clever and will soon cotton on to the idea of night and day. By six weeks old, they should start to get an idea of the difference between night and daytime and, combined with a good routine, this will contribute to a good sleep pattern.

Day time naps

Some parents think that if a baby doesn't sleep during the day it will be more tired at night and thus sleep longer and better, No! This is wrong, in fact the total opposite happens!

Babies that don't have regular naps during the day are grouchy, grumbly and overtired; therefore waking lots in the night.

Getting your child into good sleep habits can only really be achieved after a good daily routine is established. Without a good daily routine, and this goes for a baby or child of any age, getting a little one to sleep through the night is near impossible.

In the early part of its life, up to twelve months old, a child should have a short morning nap, and a longer two to three hour nap in the afternoon.

Cut out the morning naps at around 12 months, and finally all naps between the ages of two and three, depending on how your little ones feel.

A good bedtime routine

A good routine doesn't end at bedtime, if anything, it starts at bedtime! It's important to get into a good bedtime routine from a very early age. You should start as you mean to go on!

Bedtime should start the minute you are upstairs getting your little ones ready to go to bed.

Start with a nice bath! Have lots of fun in the bath with toys, bubbles and singing time. Even from a very young age this is important! Sing to your babies in the bath, trickle water over them and make fun sounds. The longer and more fun, the better! Encourage your children to interact with each other – bath time is a great bonding time for all of you!

> **Just as adults do, children like to know when the fun is going to stop, so warn them in advance that bath time is going to end #TwoMinuteWarning #ExpectoGetWet**

Always prepare your older children for the idea that bath time is nearly over by giving them a two minute warning. Sounds silly? Not at all – and abrupt end to fun is often where tantrums start. Children who don't have time to get used to the idea that something enjoyable is about to end can break into floods of tears, which turns bedtime into a nightmare!

After their bath, dry all your little ones with nice, big fluffy towels – making it lots of fun! Sing songs, and cuddle them dry! Giving all your children equal tickles and attention can be hard, but so important. Make sure their pyjamas are in the bathroom or close by and when they are dry, dress them, talking all the time about snuggly bedtime or the bedtime book you are all going to read together.

Keep using the word bedtime, or sleepy time, to encourage the idea that this is in fact bedtime – not playtime!

In their bedroom, snuggle everyone up together with a book,

babies will usually have their bedtime milk or feed at this point. After the story, get your child into bed, tuck them in and say goodnight.

It's worth investing in a big beanbag for this so you can all snuggle together. Although I don't have twins I do have two that were born less than a year apart, so having big cushions to all snuggle together on was great for bedtime stories. Especially when they were both not walking!

Older children

If, at the end of story time they have got into bed DO NOT enter into a conversation about another story, the idea that they may need a drink, a wee or to play with their toys! My two love bedtime but they also love their stalling tactics. Working together as a team is something twins, triplets and children close in age can pick up easily when it comes to bad bedtimes – stay strong and be firm but fair.

Just repeat that it's bedtime, and keep taking them back to bed. I have to admit that I've struggled not to giggle on many occasions when mine have had their tricky nights, working together as a troublesome two at bedtime. It soon becomes boring for them though - when you are not entering into conversation and just taking them back to bed saying the same thing!

As exhausting as that technique is, it really works. With two or more, it just takes a little longer and you may need back up from your partner or family while you are sleep training.

> **Twins, triplets and children close in age quickly learn to work in teams, but you can't give in to them at bedtime, no matter how cute their requests #JustOneMoreStory**

CHAPTER 6

EXTRA SPECIAL HAPPY BABY BEDTIMES

Over the past 21 years I've worked with lots of wonderful children and babies who had extra special needs. More recently a very good friend of mine asked for my advice when caring for her little boy, Noah, who was born with Spina Bifida and Hydrocephalus.

"Our son Noah has Spina Bifida and Hydrocephalus and he has only two per cent of a normal sized brain," explained my friend Shelley Wall. " Being a social media user we saw you give out expert advice, but we wanted to have your help via email to keep things private.

"Eventually, having chatted via twitter initially, we were happy that your methods would be suitably gentle for our needs and Noah's. Using the gentle approach suited Noah."

Shelley and her husband Rob are the parents of three lovely children and Noah is the youngest. "We think all parents and children are individuals so we were looking for individual advice aimed at our very individual set of circumstances," continued Shelley. "There are lots of experts out there, especially on Twitter, offering general advice but we needed something specifically tailored to our needs.

"Our advice to any parent would be that, if you need help, get in touch with Fi and just have a chat. She is very professional, she gives great advice and genuinely cares about helping your little ones and you resolve the problems you may be having. She has a very gentle and loving approach. Having seen on Twitter how Fi deals with questions from parents, I can testify that she wears her heart on her sleeve."

Sleep problems in disabled children are very common, which means that parents who are already tired from the extra responsibility of dealing with their little one's special needs often find themselves physically and emotionally exhausted after reduced sleep.

As with the majority of sleep cases that come to me, there are a number of reasons why your little one may not be sleeping and so it's essential to find the actual problem, before attempting any of my sleep training techniques.

Firstly, let's talk about babies with special needs. I've worked with lots of families over the years whose little ones have special needs. This has given me the opportunity to develop my techniques in a way that works for very little ones.

For babies with special needs establishing a routine can be difficult. For example, medication, hospital visits and the frequent ups and downs of their condition all make it hard to keep an hour by hour routine in place. For these reasons I'd suggest sticking as best possible to a gentle and easy routine that fits in with your life.

Routine is the magic key to happy baby bedtimes…

What do I mean when I say routine? I mean feeding, bedtime, nap-times and regular daily activities. Many special needs babies have spent time in hospital at the beginning of their life and so a routine is often already in place. It's a really good idea to stick to this routine and continue it at home if possible. To change an already working feeding, medication and nap routine isn't advisable and can cause all kinds of problems - so stick to the times for feeding as best you can. Simply adapt it as they grow older and their needs change.

Even from a very young age your babies will thrive on routine and a regular morning outing to the park or meeting other parents and babies can be a productive part of that. I think it is really beneficial for parents to meet other parents in similar circumstances to get together with their little ones. Ask your Health Visitor for a list of local groups, or your hospital should have information on services and groups available to you in your area.

In short - regular feeding times and regular nap and bedtimes are the key to happy baby bedtimes. So if for any reason your routine gets out of wack, due to a hospital stay or break away for example, try and get back to the routine as soon as you can.

As a parent of two little ones who have frequent hospital stays – I know how easy it is to fall out of routine and how quickly that change effects their sleep. It's essential to get back to routine.

It's incredibly difficult to promise a parent a happy sleeper but by following my techniques, as they are described in this book, there is hope. It's an even harder promise to make, when the baby in question has additional needs, but I firmly believe a good routine works with *all* babies and that it will help you and your little one cope with the difficulties that often arise when caring for a child with extra needs.

Finding the reason for wakefulness

With older children, there are a variety of reasons they might suffer from night wakings or refuse to go to sleep in the first instance. It's quite possible that because of your child's special needs, they will be unable to communicate those reasons to you. However, you don't have to rely entirely on guesswork or intuition to work out they are.

Temperature - Is your child to hot or cold?

Think about what your child wears to bed - are they too cold or too hot to sleep? You need to make the decision for them if there is limited communication. Take their temperature, check for red cheeks or sweatiness and feel their skin to see if its clammy or sweaty. It's also worthwhile investing in a good quality, reliable, digital baby thermometer. This will also be invaluable when your child is ill - if only to reassure you that their temperature isn't too high.

You should think about where your little one's bed is positioned. Is it close to a heater? Near a draughty window? What about the bed itself? Is the duvet tog too thick or too thin? Think about how you sleep in your bed and compare it to your child's bed and bedclothes.

Is your child hungry or thirsty?

Are they good eaters, who tick into a generous serving every mealtime, or super snackers who graze little and often? Do they have a drink and snack before bed? If not, perhaps they need to. Think of their age - have you increased their portion sizes as they have grown? Do you think they are eating enough in the day? Is their diet balanced and filling? Are they dehydrated? How much do they drink?

Many older children with disabilities are incontinent and this can be a common cause of disrupted sleep. It's worth investing in some good night-time incontinence pants. For younger children, up to ten, there are some fantastic night-time pants that provide hours of protection and comfort by keeping them dry thus avoiding disrupted sleep caused by wetness.

Other than their regular health problems, is your child poorly?

Often there are silent viruses that don't show many symptoms. In winter months particularly there are coughs and colds and horrid viruses that can leave your child feeling poorly without clear symptoms. Regularly check their temperature and give them infant paracetamol to reduce any raised temperatures or discomfort. Of course, you should always check with your pharmacist that painkillers are compatible with any current medication your little one is having before giving infant paracetamol or infant ibuprofen.

Is your child happy where they sleep?

Think about your child's room in particular their bed. Have they grown too big for a toddler bed? Is their bed too hard? Or too soft? Does it not offer enough support?

Are the bed sheets fitted well? Many children hate crumpled sheets. As silly as it sounds it can make them uncomfortable and stop them sleeping.

Next it's time to address the quilt. Is it comfortable? What about the pattern, is it too busy? Too bright? What is it washed in? Remember, many fabric powders can irritate skin.

Is the room dark enough? Even low lights can disturb light sleepers. Sleeping in the dark is the best way to sleep. But as a mum of two children who don't like the dark, I understand that there is a flip side to talk about. Is it too dark? Many children have night fears - so a soft night light can help.

If your child is afraid of the dark a night light or light projector can be incredibly comforting, especially for a little one with special needs. They don't need to be expensive and eco-friendly ones that are kind to the environment, and to your energy bill, are available.

Just as the position of your littlie's bed is important when establishing whether their temperature is a problem, it can also be an issue with regard to their general comfort in the room. Is the bed too close to the door where noises can disturb them? Is it positioned in such a way that they can see all of their room. We all remember how the bogey man seemed able to hide in the smallest shadow.

Night fears are very real to a child and one who is worried but can't communicate their fears will feel so much more secure in a bed close to a wall that allows them to see the whole of their room.

"Night fears are very real to a child and one who is worried but can't communicate their fears will feel so much more secure in a bed close to a wall that allows them to see the whole of their room."

How is the room decorated? Are there toys in the room? Is it too exciting an environment to sleep in? I've had many parents who came back to me to thank me for the simple suggestion that they remove the toys from their little one's bedroom at night. Sleep problems solved instantly!

Is your child too excited or too over-stimulated to sleep?

In this wonderful generation of smartphones and tablets - many little ones are spending lots of time online or playing games. The right games and applications can be very positive and educational, even for quite young children, but there are also many dangers. Amongst these is over-stimulation before bed.

I'd always advise parents to stop any TV, tablet or mobile use at least an hour before bed to enable a allow for a good wind-down. Instead, create a calming hour of bath, story and bed.

The daily routine

It's essential that your child has plenty of activity in the day because a lack of stimulation can cause sleep problems. You should ensure that their daily routine provides as much physically stimulating activity as possible in both the morning and the afternoon, within the constraints of your child's special needs.

If your child is older than two or three, depending on the child, you will find that a nap no longer helps them sleep during the night. My son is three and he currently takes very occasional naps for no longer than an hour in the afternoon and never sleeping later than half past three. His bedtime is six o'clock.

If you, he or she is having problems sleeping, your child will be tired from being awake early in the morning or from not getting enough sleep at night. But letting them nap in the day won't help their night time problems.

Unlike babies whose naps actually aid night time sleep, older children don't really need naps in the day. Of course there's the problem of keeping them awake if they have woken very early, but try. Even if you can restrict them to dozing for just ten minutes it will be better than a full hour long nap.

Eventually cutting that nap will make a huge difference at bedtime. Also make sure other care providers, such as nurseries, schools, relatives or respite providers know that this is what you are doing.

Bedtime routine

Routine really is the magic key and many special needs children in particular thrive on it. Ensure, as much as you possibly can, that the daily routine and bedtime routine stay the same.

You should address the simple things first. Keep meal times to a regular time and keep bedtime to the same hour each night. Of course life doesn't always make this easy, but when something happens that drags you away from your routine always get back to it as soon as you can.

What if, after addressing all of these issues my child still won't settle? Well, then, and only then, should you use some of my gentle sleep training techniques.

Many children with special needs thrive on routine. If the routine gets messed up – get back to it as soon as you can #RoutineisTheMagicKey

CHAPTER 7

THINGS THAT GO BUMP IN THE NIGHT

Monsters are a big problem in our house. Little Betsy and Oscar are sometimes afraid at night, partly because of their obsession with monster games in the day and monster stories. My husband and I are quite good at fighting off monsters now though and we make the littlies laugh with delight when we turf out a ghoul or two that's been hiding under the bed. Even their godparents have got in on the act, with Uncle Phil shouting upstairs, telling the monsters to, "be gone or else!" to the delight of the little ones!

Betsy and Oscar's fears are completely normal though. I had them as a child and I'm willing to bet that you did too. Even brave Uncle Phil had them and he's a professional monster catcher, as far as Betsy and Oscar are concerned. Of course, in day today life he moonlights as a car salesman.

As parents and caregivers, we just have to give our littlies love and hugs, and entertain their fears, rather than telling them they are being silly. So scare the monsters away, shoo them out of the cupboards and drive them from your shadows. Your children will appreciate you for it and sleep sounder and longer. And when they grow up, looking back on it they will love and appreciate you all the more.

I feel quite strongly on this subject and I understand that entertaining the idea that monsters exist is risky. But telling a young child, 'it's not real' won't help them; because to them monsters are *very* real.

My two are at an age when their vivid little imaginations are developing quickly, and nightmares are frequent and unwelcome visitors. Little ones often distort reality during sleep and in their dreams. For example, a funny book your little one read with you during the day can morph into a monster mash in a dream. For a little person that can be quite terrifying as they often don't understand that what they saw in their nightmare or terror wasn't real.

Never ignore your little one's fears or nightmares, whatever they are about. A fear of the dark is common in children, so let them sleep with a night-light or hallway light on. It really doesn't matter as long as they are happy to stay in bed and sleep soundly with the light on. When they are feeling more confident you can agree with them that they should start sleeping without the nightlight on.

Remember, to them the fears are very real. By becoming a monster fighter and helping them with their fears, you are helping them to feel safe and manage their feelings.

> **It might sound crazy to play along with monster fears, by hunting ghouls in the cupboards and scaring ghosts away from under the stairs, but real actions help your children with the fears that seem real to them #MonstersBeGone**

There are lots of things you can do in the day to help assuage your little one's monster fears. We take part in lots of role play games, have arty fun making monster masks, or cook up monster meals. The key is to talk all about your little one's fears throughout the games. Change the nightmares into daydreams and the scary thoughts into friendly ones.

At the same time it's important not to make them *too* real and its essential you never use your child's fears against them. 'Tidy your toys away or the monsters will be cross,' is the worst thing you can say and a sure way of saying hello to sleepless nights for a good few weeks!

Fear of the dark

Fear of the dark is extremely common in little ones, and, although many studies have shown that children and adults sleep better in the dark - because it allows our senses to completely turn off, it's more important to feel comfortable.

I suggest to parents whose little ones have suddenly developed a fear of the dark to invest in a nice night light, one that's not too bright, or to allow your little one to have their door open and leave the hallway light on.

My two were fantastic sleepers in the dark until they were around two years old. At the age where imaginations develop and run wild at night-time. It was no surprise to me that they suddenly wanted a light on. And they still do.

However, they have gone from lamps on in their room, to doors open a little with the bathroom light on - glowing just enough to reassure them but not keep them awake.

These fears are very real for little ones and it's so important to address them, rather than dismiss them. You may find after a few weeks they are ready to sleep in the dark again but if not don't worry. It takes time and lots of patience to work through fears.

Night terrors and nightmares

Night terrors

Sadly all children will have a night terror or nightmare at some point during their life. It's a horrid, scary and worrying thing to go through for both parent and child. But not many people know that a nightmare and night terror are two different things.

What's the difference between a night terror and nightmare?

A night terror, also known as a sleep terror, affects younger children and causes awful feelings of terror or dread. A night terror typically occurs in the first half hour to hour of sleep.

Though night terrors can be alarming and often worrying, they're not usually cause for concern or a sign of a deeper medical issue.

Littlies who have night terrors usually shout out or scream in their sleep, sit or stand up, and have a look of fear on their face. Betsy is often covered in sweat, which is a classic sign of a night terror. Children experiencing a night terror will usually sweat, breathe fast and have a rapid heart rate.

As a parent it's a horrible thing to witness but the important thing is to remain calm. Hold your little one close and, if they wake fully, reassure them.

What causes night terrors?

Get ready for the the sciencey bit. Night terrors are caused by over-arousal of the central nervous system during sleep. This may happen because the central nervous system, which regulates sleep and waking brain activity, is still maturing so it goes a little, well, silly.

Night terrors are most commonly triggered by being extremely overtired, so ensure your little one has a good routine and, if they are under three, ensure they are having at least an hours rest time or nap during the day. For older children, try and get them to have some quiet time - this could be looking at books on their bed, or quiet time watching TV.

Sometimes change can cause night terrors; for instance, sleeping in a new bed or being away from home. Starting school or nursery can also trigger a night terror, so be prepared and try not to worry.

What can I do?

The best possible way to handle night terrors is to comfort and reassure your little one and snuggle them back down into their bed. With night terrors, children tend to wake up confused and often slip back to sleep quite quickly.

It's tempting to pick up your child and take them into your room, but it's really important to keep them in their own bed. Bad habits are easily made - and a child who is used to sleeping all night in their own bed will suddenly not want to sleep there anymore if you create the idea that they can sleep in yours.

Stay with your child until they are calm and their breathing is settled. Stroke their head and cuddle them back into bed. It's important to let them get back to sleep themselves - don't be tempted to rock, cuddle or stroke them to sleep. Stay with them until they are asleep if you wish, but save the rocking and cuddling for the waking hours.

Nightmares

Nightmares are bad dreams that cause upset and fear and are quite common in young children. They usually occur at some point after one and a half hours of sleep.

If your little one has had a nightmare they will find it hard to get back to sleep. They will be very distressed and upset and, in extreme cases, find settling at night very difficult because they will be worried that the nightmare is going to return.

When nightmares become more frequent or occur on a regular basis, it may be a sign of stress in your child's life or environment. Don't panic! This doesn't necessarily mean something terrible and traumatic, it can be something as simple as changing class, moving house or starting a new school.

What causes nightmares?

Would you believe it? The thing my Nanna warned me about was true! 'Don't eat before bed or you'll have bad dreams!' While researching night terrors for my book, I discovered that eating before bed triggers an increase in the body's metabolism and brain activity. Thus, in turn, causing nightmares.

The loss of a relative or pet and family separations can also be the cause of persistent nightmares. If you feel that one of these reasons could be the root of your child's sleep issues, it's important to address them in the day by talking, drawing, reading and reassuring them during, what will inevitably be, a difficult time.

Nightmares can also be the result of reading or watching frightening things before bed. So, while I'd not like to discourage bedtime stories, I'd advise steering clear of frightening books with older children and monster stories for very young children – especially if they have started to have nightmares.

What can I do?

If you have suffered a nightmare yourself, you will probably remember the feelings of worry and fear you experience afterwards. Sometimes bad dreams seem very real and can be terribly upsetting.

The best possible way to handle nightmares is to cuddle and reassure your little one and snuggle them back down in their bed. Make them feel safe again and talk through the dream with them if - they can remember it.

It's really important to remember here, as with night terrors, to keep your child in their own bed because bad habits are easily made!

> **Bad habits are easily made, so never let you child come into your bed after nightmares or night terrors**
> **#HappyBabyBedTime**

Stay with your child until they are calm and their breathing is settled. Stroke their head and cuddle them back into bed. As mentioned before, it's really important to let them get back to sleep themselves – don't be tempted to rock, cuddle or stroke them to sleep.

Read books about bad dreams and reassure your child that their experiences are normal and nothing to worry about.

And remember, maintaining a good bedtime routine is essential in getting a good night's sleep. Regular bath time, stories, snuggles and lights-out each night will reassure and calm your child before bed.

Try not to worry about nasties in the night. It is distressing as a parent to see our children have night terrors and nightmares, but remember that nightmares and night terrors pass and they are part of childhood. #NightmaresBeGone

CHAPTER 8

DON'T CRY LITTLE ONE!

What is controlled crying?

Controlled crying, also called control crying, means checking on your child at set intervals, increasing the time between visits until they fall asleep. I'm not a huge fan of this technique but I wanted to include it in my book, so that, if *you* want to use it, you can do so in the correct way and not they way I've seen it described in other sleep guides and on some web sites. Some of these, quite frankly, really concern me. It's particularly worrying when controlled crying is disguised as a gentle method; I've even heard it called controlled comforting. But crying is crying.

How do I use controlled crying?

After you have ensured your baby is clean, dry and fed, put the little one to bed in their cot and leave the room. If they cry, don't return until one minute has passed. When it has, go back into the room, gently whisper 'sleepy time' and stroke their tummy for two minutes. Then leave.

The idea is not for you to get your child back to sleep, but to reassure yourself and your baby that all is well. You then increase the interval between visits by a further minute each time, starting with two minutes and going up to a maximum of 10 minutes.

Keep repeating the process until your child quietens down and goes to sleep. If you are committed to it and want it to work, you must also use this technique if your child wakes repeatedly in the night. It's important to mention here that controlled crying shouldn't be used if children have serious health problems or even if they are just feeling poorly.

Controlled crying isn't everyone's cup of tea

As with all parenting techniques, it is a matter of opinion which techniques are mostly likely to work and which aren't in any individual example. It's never a case of one size fits all when it comes to children. But I wanted my book to show you all the methods used, even if some of them are disapproved of by me, other professionals or other parents. I wanted to show you how to use them correctly.

All children are unique individuals who will grow in their own way of life and respond differently to different techniques. It's never a one size fits all approach when it comes to parenting.

During my 20 year professional career, and as a mum of two little ones, I have used controlled crying when a situation has arisen in which I need to. For example when a child is inconsolable and overtired. However, I do think it should be a last resort and that routine can solve nearly any sleep problems that may arise in normal circumstances.

Leaving a baby crying for long periods of time is not right or fair on them and can have a negative effect. But for periods of up to ten minutes, controlled crying techniques are safe. The key with any technique is using it properly and not abusing it.

In 2010 Dr Penelope Leach caused outrage among healthcare and childcare professionals when she claimed that recent scientific tests show high levels of the stress hormone cortisol develop in babies when no one answers their cries.

If this happens over long periods and repeatedly, it can be

"toxic" to their brains. However, this was based on crying for periods of thirty minutes and more, not in controlled environments where control crying techniques are used.

In contrast, another recent study showed that controlled crying had no adverse affects.

At the Murdoch Children's Research Institute in Australia, 225 six-year-old children were studied. All these children had received behavioural sleep intervention as babies to assess their health – including emotional well-being, behaviour and child-parent relationship.

This study found that techniques such as controlled crying had no adverse affects on the emotional and behavioural development of children or on their relationship with parents.

So what are we to do? Do we let our babies cry? Or do we pick them up and strap them to us every time they whimper?

As a mother and a professional I think it's all about balance. Recognising your baby's cry is something that comes quite quickly and understanding their needs and responding accordingly will come naturally to many.

If you are struggling to recognise the difference in your baby's cry – get in touch with your Health Visitor, who will be able to offer clear guidance. If I could pop a few sound bites into this book, it would be so much easier to explain the different cries!

CHAPTER 9

SNUG AS A BUG

When parents ask me to help them with their unhappy sleeper, I always ask for a description of the room and surroundings in which their child sleeps. Why? Because the sleeping environment, in particular the cot or crib, is very important.

Often something as simple as little one being too hot or too cold can disrupt sleep, as can too much light through a window, or, as one family I helped discovered, the grumble of the boiler system turning on everyday at 5am.

So how do you create a happy bedtime baby's room?

We all get excited when we become pregnant and it's easy to

go overboard on room decoration and accessories. But the really important thing to remember when kitting out little one's room isn't the candy striped bunting or the fluffy bunny collection. It's comfort.

In order to have a happy bedtime baby sleeper, they need to be comfortable.

To make it a little easier to understand I'm going to break the room down into sections because, my lovelies, there is much to learn when it comes to comfy, happy babies and little ones.

We have already talked about baby routines and bedtime routines and how important they are for a happy sleeper, but comfort is just as important.

Can you imagine being wrapped up really tightly in a sleep suit, a sleeping bag and a quilt and still feeling comfy? No, me neither, but so many parents do this to their babies, thinking they are keeping them snug as a bug in a rug. What they are actually doing is over-heating their baby and it's not only uncomfortable for baby, it's very dangerous.

Without wanting to frighten you too much, I'm going to talk here about SIDS (Sudden Infant Death Syndrome) commonly known as cot death. One of the causes associated with SIDS is the over-heating of babies.

Let's talk room temperature

An ideal room temperature for your baby is between 16-20°C. To achieve this, it's a good idea to buy a room thermometer or baby monitor which has temperature as a built in feature.

Remember that seasons change the room temperature. In summer you have to ensure the room doesn't get too hot and the winter that it doesn't get too cold. Ironically, it's tempting to wack up the heating in Winter, but this, together with warmer winter clothes and bedding can cause overheating.

In the summer, if you need to open windows, ensure it is safe to do so and avoid leaving them open when baby is in the room. A fan is a good investment, but you must ensure you keep it out of baby's reach. And remember don't direct the fan towards the baby.

Look out for draughts in the room, especially in older houses. Avoid placing a cot near a window as in the Winter it can make baby too cold and in the summer, when the sun shines through it can make baby too hot for its daytime nap.

Let's talk bedding!

There is so much cutesy, cosy bedding available out there to entice parents into parting with their cash. But really all your baby needs in the early days is a fitted cot sheet, a sleeping bag and a blanket. Babies don't need quilts and really you should avoid them until your little one is old enough for a bed. Even the blanket is only needed if it is very cold and then you should ensure it is tucked in safely.

There is often debate about cot bumpers. In my honest, professional opinion I'd say avoid the bumpers. You really don't need them and they can be dangerous when baby is older and moving about. It's easy for a baby to become trapped underneath a cot bumper. For me, the emptier the crib or cot the safer the crib or cot.

You should also avoid having soft toys or mobiles hanging over the cot. Your little one really doesn't need them.

No pillows are needed for your baby. In fact, it'll be a while until you need to invest in a pillow at all. It's advisable not to use one until your little one is about two and moves from a cot into a bed. You should never have a pillow or duvet in a cot – both are associated with an increased risk of SIDS.

Let's talk cot sheets

A well fitted cot sheet is advisable. It's worth investing in two or three spares in case of accidents and to avoid washing nightmares! It's also worth investing in a protective sheet to avoid any accidents soaking through to the mattress.

Let's talk sleeping bags

There are lots of sleeping bags available, in different togs and different sizes. I love sleeping bags because they help baby avoid getting too cold in the night. We had quite a varied range of sleeping bags for winter and summer as well as different bags for different ages. We used them right up until the littlies could walk and it kept them cosy. Once your child can walk and you move them onto a bed, it's time to put the sleeping bags into your memory box and move on to blankets or a duvet.

We never used a blanket with the sleeping bags unless it was a very cold night. We are fortunate enough to have quite a warm house in the winter, so we never had the need for blankets together with a sleeping bag. However, a warning here. If you do use a blanket and a sleeping bag make sure you do the temperature checks mentioned above thoroughly. Check baby isn't overheating. If they are, it sounds obvious, but, remove the blanket!

Let's talk cots and beds

We've talked about room temperature and bedding to avoid baby getting too hot or too cold, so now we'll talk beds.

From birth it's advisable that your baby sleeps in a cot or crib in your room for the first six months.

Of course this isn't ideal in all homes, and it doesn't always work, especially if you or your partner are loud sleepers (I'm talking snoring! Anyone else have a snorer?)

Where your baby sleeps is very important. It must be clean, warm and above all safe. In the early days a crib is advisable, and practical, because you can move it around your home so that your baby is always near you.

When you are ready to move on from the cot, it's worth really investing in a good quality bed and buying a good mattress to go in it. Choose a mattress that's firm, rather than soft, and that fits well in the cot with no gaps around the edges. Always use a new mattress for a new baby. Even if your baby has a sibling, don't be tempted to use their old mattress.

It's also worth thinking about getting a cot bed in the first instance – that way it'll last you way beyond the baby years! A cot bed is a cot that adapts into a bed as your baby grows up and becomes a toddler. It's well worth investing in a cot-bed as it could last you from birth right up to five years!

As well as considering the design and look, ensure the cot you choose conforms to British Safety Standards (BSEN716). The rules are regulations are there for a reason and they will help keep baby safe!

> **Time to get techy. Choose a cot that complies with British Safety Standard (BSEN716) because the rules are there for a reason and keep baby safe #BabySleepGeek**

When planning your baby's room, ensure the cot isn't near a radiator or sunny window. Babies are less able to regulate their body temperature so may overheat quickly. I keep harking back to this but it's one of the most common causes of sleep problems. Blind cords are also a risk to babies, so ensure they aren't near the cot, or preferably just use cordless blinds.

Let's talk SIDS

I've mentioned Sudden Infant Death Syndrome briefly in a previous chapter, but now I'm going explain to you in more detail about how important it is to have your baby sleep on their backs.

All the evidence from every source around the world suggests that placing your baby on their back at the beginning of every sleep or nap significantly reduces the risk of SIDS.

If your baby is in a cot, make sure they can't wriggle down under the blanket by putting them in the 'feet to foot' position with their feet at the bottom of the cot, rather than their head at the top. Don't use a pillow, as I've already mentioned babies don't need a pillow until they are one year old. And finally, never risk falling asleep with your baby on a sofa or armchair.

By following these simple steps from The Lullaby Trust, you'll be taking the most proactive measures you can to ensure your baby is sleeping as safely as possible:

- *You should always place your baby on their back to sleep and not on their front or side - unless your doctor has advised you of a medical reason to do so*
- *If your baby has rolled onto their tummy, you should turn them onto their back again*
- *Once your baby can roll from back to front and back again, on their own, they can be left to find their own position*

The information isn't intended to frighten you, it's simply a guide to help parents avoid the dangers associated with SIDS.

Co-sleeping has been debated a good deal over the past few years, with many people believing that babies who co-sleep are at a higher risk of SIDS.

As someone who lost a sibling to SIDS, I have been aware of the problem from a young age. I keep track of any new research, and I always follow the up to date NHS guidelines rigidly with my own children and advise parents who contact me to do the same. Having said that, I also understand that many parent still want to co-sleep. So it is important to me to include safer ways of co-sleeping in this book rather than dismissing the concept entirely.

The Department of Health advises that bed-sharing should be avoided if one or both parents is a smoker, has consumed alcohol or has taken any drugs, prescription or otherwise, that affect perception, cause drowsiness or affect depth of sleep.

They also say that you should avoid co-sleeping if you are excessively tired to the extent that this might affect being able to respond to the baby.

The risks of co-sleeping are also increased if your baby:

- Was born prematurely (37 weeks or less)
- Had a low birth weight (less than 2.5kg or 5.5lb)
- Has a fever or any signs of illness

If you do decide to co-sleep, you need to make sure your baby can't fall out of bed and keep your baby cool by using sheets and blankets rather than a duvet. Furthermore, just as if it were in their own bed, always put your baby to sleep on its back rather than its front or side.

If you are worried at all about the risks of co-sleeping but still want to be close to your baby, there are cot-beds available which slot snugly onto your own bed frame. I believe these are far better than having your baby in bed with you and still allow you to enjoy the benefits of co-sleeping.

These 'bay cot beds' offer the benefits of co-sleeping while providing a safe, separate sleeping environment for one or two babies that is only an arm's reach away from the parent for comforting, feeding and bonding.

> **Bay cot beds offer the comfort of co-sleeping but remove much of the danger. It's down to you to choose how to care for your baby and if you want to co-sleep, think safety #Live&LetLive**

Let's talk monitors

If you are planning on putting your little ones straight into their own room, for whatever reason, it's important to invest in a good monitor. However, I have to advise here that NHS guidelines suggest your baby is safest in your room with you until they are six months old.

We used the Angel Care monitor system for both Betsy and Oscar. We still use them now for reassurance. It's good to be able to hear when they have had a nightmare so you can reassure them right away. Similarly, if they are poorly or just need help with going to the toilet in the night, it's good to know.

A monitor with heartbeat detection provides extra safety for your baby if they are not sleeping in your room or bed. They are also fantastic for when baby has naps upstairs and you are downstairs checking emails or doing mundane chores! It's an extra step towards keeping baby safe while sleeping and also gives you peace of mind.

Many baby monitors also feature temperature sensors to keep an eye on baby's comfort and health. But, if you are unsure how hot or cold your baby is, check their tummy. Hands and feet are often cold so don't use them as a guide. Remember also that babies who are poorly will be much hotter. We'll cover illness later in more detail, but signs of overheating to look out for are a sweaty or clammy body and redness of face or body.

> **If your little one has a sweaty or clammy body or a red face or body it's a sign of overheating #KeepthatTempDown**

CHAPTER 10

BYE-BYE BABY BED

There is no set-in-stone rule for when you should move from cot to bed, but the majority of little ones make the move sometime between ages 18 months and three and a half years old.

My two both went into beds when they just turned two. With bed guards, they felt happy and safe and we never had any trouble at all. Bed guards are a nice gentle way of reassuring little ones who have moved from the four sided safety of a cot into a single bed.

I would always advise investing in a bed guard, as leaving the safety of a cot and going straight into a bed with no sides can lead to accidents. You can remove the guards once you think they are not going to roll out.

To ease the transition from cot to bed, always put the new bed in the place of the cot – this way they'll not be dealing with a change of bed and a change of room or view from their regular sleeping position. It's tempting to buy new bedding to go with the new bed, but it's a better idea to keep the old bedding and change once they are settled into their new environment. Too much change can cause sleep problems and unhappy bedtimes.

Many parents decide to move their child to a bed when they feel they have outgrown the cot – and that's fine. But the arrival of another baby is also one of the most common reasons to make the move and this might need extra thought. If the reason for the move is that you're having another baby, make the switch at least three months before the new sibling is due to arrive. This way your older child won't feel turfed out of their old bed!

You want your older child to take time to adjust to their new bed. A disrupted night caused by both the newborn and an unhappy sibling who doesn't want to be in a strange bed isn't going to be a happy baby bedtime time at all!

Parents often make the move to a bed when their little ones discover they can get out of their cot. I'd have to agree that this is a sure sign that your little one is ready to say goodbye to their baby bed. Don't ignore constant cot climbing – it's far better to move to a bed than have any unwanted bumps in the night!

Finally, if your little one has started toilet training, it's much easier to attempt night wees if they are in a bed rather than a cot.

Irrespective of the reason that makes you decide to move from cot to bed, be prepared for a few disturbed nights sleep. It's a new thing for your little one; sometimes it's exciting and sometimes it's upsetting. Be understanding and help your little one love their new bed by investing time into helping them settle. Reward their efforts when they stay in their new bed by telling them how proud you are of them.

Some children will adjust easily to the change, while others will not. Every child is different, so don't worry if it takes a little longer than expected.

> **Every child is different, so when your little one moves to a new bed, give them time to settle in at their own pace #BigBoyBed #BigGirlBed**

If your little one starts to make appearances downstairs, now they don't have the bars of the cot to keep them in bed, simply return them to bed; telling them gently that it's bedtime. Start as you mean to go on. If you let them stay downstairs, or climb into your bed once or twice, you'll find it incredibly hard to stop them leaving their beds before morning time in the future.

If you are having trouble with your little one who has just moved from cot to bed – this next chapter is for you!

CHAPTER 11

OLDER BABY BEDTIMES (TODDLERS+)

You might be reading this book because your usual, happy sleeper has suddenly decided to keep you up at night as they get older. You might have never had a contented little one at night and the problems your child displayed as a baby are still as bad as ever. Either way, this book can help with your wakeful toddler and older child as well as your baby and this chapter is where I'm going to do exactly that.

I'll be talking about sleep problems associated with older children, such as nightmares and night terrors, night fears and early risers.

If you've just read over that paragraph and are suddenly quite worried that your happy bedtime baby is going to turn into a nightmare toddler, please don't worry. Sleep problems can happen at any age and anytime – so what was once a peaceful baby who slept well can suddenly become a night owl.

> **Sleep problems can happen at any age – night owl toddlers and early riser schoolies are just as common as wakeful babies and restless littlies #PasstheCoffee**

The solution to any sleep problem is finding the cause and dealing with it; eventually getting back to a good bedtime and saying goodnight to sleepless nights again.

For example, my two perfect sleepers once came back from a two week family holiday as THE worst sleepers I could imagine. They found it hard to settle, they woke early and they had disturbed nights. Coffee was my best friend on those awful mornings after the nights before.

Their problem was the break in routine. Routine is the key to a good night's sleep and when your baby turns into a toddler, routine remains very important. In fact, routine is important all the way through our life - if we want to sleep well. Even as adults a regular bedtime is great for our body-clock and helps us our brain to switch off at bedtime.

Routines for toddlers and older children

Did you know that children aged one to three typically need between twelve and 14 hours per day. Three to six year olds need ten to twelve hours per day and seven to nine year old children need between ten and eleven hours per day. Yet the majority of children whose parents come to me in the beginning are getting just over half that! That's quite a worry isn't it? Sleep is so important.

I believe that sleep is just as important for children's development as healthy eating and regular exercise because it plays a significant role in brain development. As well as development, sleep also plays an important role in your little one's daily ability to function.

As adults we have all experienced, at some point, what a lack of sleep can do right? Putting the milk in the dishwasher and the bread in the microwave? No? Just me with those sleep deprivation mistakes?

A lack of sleep makes it so much harder to concentrate. It can make us irritable, clumsy and grumpy. For older children attending a whole day of school or nursery it creates a grumpy, often disruptive child. Not ideal.

Let's be honest - Toddlers are a lively bunch of awesome. I love the toddler years – the fun, energetic sparkle my two toddlers bring to the world makes me smile and makes my heart burst. But take away their regular daily routine or add some sleepless nights and, oh boy, they are no fun. They are irritable, grumpy and nothing makes them happy. Not even cake and everyone loves cake right?

> **Cake solves most things, but not even cake can make up for a toddler losing a night's sleep #ExpectaGrumpster #CakeisHappiness**

My two are a delight because of routine. Even though they no longer need their meals at the exact same time of day everyday, like they did as babies, there is still an element of routine. For example, they eat within an hour's time frame each day. That routine is essential in their lives and has a knock on effect on their sleep. So, even with older children routine is STILL the key. (Remember back in chapter one? It's the same mantra!)

The same goes for the rest of the time – every afternoon my two settle down for a movie to recharge, ready for some more afternoon activities before the wind-down to bedtime. It's just like the naps they had as babies.

The bedtime routine hasn't changed at all – Betsy and Oscar

even still have milk before bed; although now it's in a cup and it's cow's milk. The bedtime routine remains the same as it was when they were babies. Bath, stories and milk and then into bed.

I can't stress enough here that, as our little ones grow into older children, the routine is still very much an important part of their lives.

Routine, routine, routine
#CouldSheStopBangingOnAboutRoutine?
#ItMustBeQuiteImportantIfSheSaysitThisMuch?

Often parents that come to me with older children who can't, or won't, sleep simply need to change their routine. They think that now their little ones are no longer babies, it's fine to lose the routine. They drop the bedtime routine or drop regular mealtimes for instance – but that's where problems start.

It's not just routine change that can stop happy bedtimes – there are other changes that can turn happy sleepers into nightmare nappers.

A house move, a holiday away, the loss of a family member, a new sibling, a hospital stay, starting school or even something as simple as a new bed can all have an affect on sleep.

If your toddler is suddenly a wakeful one at night, think over the last paragraph? Have there been recent changes in their routine? Has something happened?

If the answer is yes, then often talking and going over the changes will make an enormous difference. Look over their routine. How can you get it back to the way it was?

One parent came to me with a child who had always been a fantastic sleeper but had suddenly developed problems. A child who slept for an average of 13 hours a night had turned into a little one that was waking up every two hours, feeling upset and climbing into bed with Mum and Dad.

After lots of questions and discussion of the routines, I discovered that the little one had had a room make-over. New bed, new decoration and new bedding. So much change!

The old quilt cover was quickly put back onto the bed for a bit of normality and happy bedtimes resumed! You see, something that seems simple and unimportant to us grown-ups can be a huge deal for little ones. So think about it, if your little one always slept well but now doesn't, there could be an answer in their routine.

Hunger is another reason for an older child not sleeping well. Just as little babies do, when older children grow, they need more sustenance. Many parents forget that their growing toddler or older child needs an increase in portion size – or more snacks in-between meals. They rarely make the connection between food and night waking or early rising. My two go through stages of not eating very much and then eating us out of house and home; so I adjust portion sizes accordingly.

Keep an eye on your child and think about their meals. Are they eating a well balanced diet? Is it enough for their age and their build? Think about bedtime – have you cut their milk but not replaced it with a bedtime drink?

Something as simple as hunger or thirst can cause lots of disruption in the night.

Illness is another cause of sleep problems in older children. Let's face it – illness keeps adults awake, so it's no surprise little ones really struggle with happy bedtimes when they are poorly.

Little ones often pick up bugs and, in the winter months, colds are a frequent occurrence in houses with young children! Sadly, this means sleepless nights and, as I have mentioned before, it's important not to use any sleep training techniques, instead simply offering comfort and care.

It's easy to bring children into your bed when they are ill and I'm guilty of this myself sometimes. There are, of course, all the safety rules to follow if you do choose to do this, but remember getting back to normal, fantastic, nights will take longer if you change the rules of sleeping. Even one or two nights in with me can result in a couple of nights of sleep training getting my two back into their own beds again! I remind myself of this when I'm tired and think it's easier to let them hop into my bed.

Having said all that, it's also important to recognise when illness has passed as many children can cotton on to the change in bedtime rules and routine and take advantage of it. My little girl is especially good at this; claiming she is still poorly quite some time after she has recovered.

> **Children can cotton on to changes in routine and try and trick Mums and Dads. Keep a watching brief! #CheekyBedtimeMonkeys**

The answer? It's difficult. You have to be certain they really are better and prepare for the fact that, following the change to their routine, it will take time to get them back to great nights again. Only you know your child well enough to determine whether they are still poorly or not.

When you are sure they are no longer ill, be firm and go back to the original bedtime routines, using the sleep training methods in chapter four. Personally, I use the bed bottom-shuffle technique after illness, just to be sure they really are better. It only takes one or two nights before we are back on track. Until the next lurgy reveals its ugly, unwelcome head that is!

Bedtime play-up

When babies are popped into bed, they can't physically get out of bed because they aren't sufficiently mobile. Toddlers who have moved to big beds and older children can though. And this is often when actually getting them into bed in the first place becomes a battle!

Again I have to say that routine is the key, ensuring your children have a good daily routine is the magic key to a good night's sleep. A good bedtime routine is essential for toddlers and older children and especially important for school age children who have long days learning.

Early risers

I've mentioned before that hunger can cause toddlers and older children to wake, but often, it's children who have never learnt to self settle who will become early risers.

When we go through the light sleep phase as adults, even if we are disturbed, we normally turn over and go back to sleep. Children and babies who have been rocked or settled to sleep with some form of 'crutch' don't have the ability to settle themselves in the same way. So they wake up fully and then, soon, their parents wake up fully as well!

Crucially though, they wake up wanting the crutch that helped them settle to sleep.

Many parents make the mistake of letting their little one get up for the day at five am. That's an awfully long day for a little one or a parent! This often results in the child wanting to nap late in the day and so the whole cycle starts again. Instead of letting your little one get up so early, you have to let the know it's still sleepy time and they need to go back to bed until it's morning time.

For older children a sleep clock is an ideal way of countering this problem. My two have a gro clock which they love. You set the time at which they are allowed to get up and the face of the clock turns from a night-time star into cheerful sunshine.

Having said that, the clock *alone* won't work. You have to take your little one back to bed when they get up too early, explain about waiting for the sunshine and repeat the process if they get up again and again until they settle. It can take a few mornings for them to understand but don't give-up or lose patience. It will work - they will understand if, and only if, you stick to it. Again you should use the same phrase and not engage in any other conversation. Simply say, "it's still sleepy time – wait for the sunshine".

For the summer months, it's advisable to invest in a good blackout blind. The early morning light wakes us all and often it's a five am burst of sunshine through the curtains that wakes a little one.

By following these tips you'll soon have a happy sleeping older child and bad nights will be a thing of the past.

> **You CAN make bad nights a thing of the past by sticking to the routines you create – whether you have tiny babies or toddlers #RoutineIsTheMagicKey**

CHAPTER 12

A HAPPY BABY BEDTIME CHECKLIST

In chapter two I covered the importance of self-settling. If your little one is normally a happy settler and suddenly won't settle, there can be a number of reasons behind it.

With babies it's more difficult to determine because they can't communicate. Here's where your happy bedtime baby checklist comes in handy. And what's awesome is it spells out thinner. Not that thinner is a winner, I just quite like a good mnemonic.

Tired?

Are they overtired? Did they miss their nap? If they are older did they have a busy day? Think through the day and pinpoint the trigger so you can work on it tomorrow.

For now it's all about using the self settling techniques in chapter four. Use the one you feel most comfortable with.

Hungry?

Is your baby having a growth spurt? Perhaps they need a food increase? Are they approaching the weaning months? Perhaps they are ready to start solid food now? Check out chapter fourteen for more information.

If they are older did they eat well at dinner time? Did they have a glass of milk before bed? With older ones I always advise a little snack and milk before bed. I'm not talking huge quantities of food, just something like a digestive biscuit and some milk.

Illness?

Do they have a raised temperature, above 34°C? Are they teething? Check the symptoms in chapter thirteen on illness.

Nappy or wind?

Is that nappy nasty? If your child is older and doesn't wear a nappy, do they need the toilet? Often sleepy children who need to go for a poo wake with a tummy ache in the night. Popping them onto the toilet and rubbing their back is a gentle way of getting them to poop while half asleep. Glamorous isn't it, this parenting life?

Sometimes, after a feed, babies will find it hard to settle due to wind. This is a common problem so don't panic, it's nothing to worry about unless they are in severe pain after a feed or always find it hard to settle after each feed, in which case it could be a sign of silent reflux. There's more information about this in our poorly baby section in the next chapter.

With wind it's important that, after each feed, you try and keep baby upright for at least 15 to 20 minutes and get some really good burps up. I'd say at least three burps, but if you can get more you'll be in for a better sleep. I'd also advise you to give small children Infacol before each night-time dream feed. It's wonderful stuff and really helps bring up the air!

No reason at all!

Sometimes children want to get out of bed for no reason at all. They are simply causing a fuss and playing up. Well, downstairs is far more interesting isn't it? When this happens, use the self settle techniques after calming and winding down for bed.

Excited?

I once received an email as part of my parent advice service that had me stumped for a little while, until I analysed the daily routine in more detail. I was frustrated as I'm rarely stumped. I can usually see the problem pretty much straight away but this family had me thinking and thinking. I'd gone through their seemingly perfect daily routine with a fine tooth comb. I was almost at a loss when I remembered the routine had said that Daddy arrived home with a treat at six pm.

According to the routine, 6.30pm was little one's bedtime.

The treat? A huge bag of chocolate buttons. Eaten in 15 minutes flat with a glass of milk, every night.

Too much sugar before bed = excitement much!

The buttons were replaced with shiny stickers and a sticker book, despite the little one's protests and the settling problem disappeared.

Another potential bedtime problem is that a lot of parents come home from work around the time that children go to be and the littlies get overexcited when they see them. My husband is guilty of this!

So, I've got the littlies all bathed and calm, their PJs are on, a story is about to start but, the second they hear the door, they shout 'Daddy!!!' jump up and down and, well, although it's lovely and they are happy, it takes quite some time to calm them and get back to our bedtime routine.

Now add to that if you will, Daddy being a monster or a pirate or an super villain and chasing them around their bedrooms. Sound familiar? Sorry Daddy and Mummy monsters out there – this is a game for mornings or afternoons, not bedtimes. It's a big cause of bedtime refusal due to over-excitement.

As exciting as it is to see a parent at the end of the day, try and get them to do the lovely hugs and kisses and then calmly read a nice story, instead of getting over excited.

Ready for bed?

A classic problem, which is particularly prevalent in slightly older little ones, is the child not getting ready for bed. As I've said, many times, routine is the key to a happy bedtime baby and a good night's sleep. Shake up the routine and little ones can easily become unsettled.

Another 'not ready for bed' problem has the parent at its root and not the child. When a little one is put to bed without a warning they may feel unready and be unwilling. This is often the case with my own two after a long journey on a weekend, they go straight to bed from the car. Their routine is already broken and they are given no warning. And it all goes wrong.

They need to be ready for bed. Children and babies thrive on routine. And routine is? OK I'll stop. I think you've got it now. (It's the key to a goodnight's sleep – just in case!)

> **A happy Baby Bedtime checklist comes in handy especially when it's a word you can remember! #thinnerchecklist**

CHAPTER 13

POORLY POPPETS

Reflux

It's 2 am, you've had very little sleep for a few days or even weeks...

In your tired arms you have a screaming, rigid-bodied baby that simply will not settle.

You've tried everything, singing, talking, walking, the chorus of Sir Mix-A-Lot's big butt song (is that only me?) and nothing will pacify your baby, who is screaming louder than you thought a tiny baby could.

Have you considered the possibility that your baby might be

suffering from reflux?

Sadly, like his older sister Betsy, Oscar developed reflux after only a week of life.

Knees raised, fists clenched, hours of crying (Oscar, not me!); I knew these familiar symptoms and took a sigh of 'oh here we go again' as I paced the room, talking and singing and watching the hours pass by...

Reflux occurs when a baby regurgitates the contents of his stomach back into the oesophagus, or mouth. Some babies won't seem bothered by the condition, while, for others, the stomach acid will burn their throat and make them uncomfortable and unsettled. For some babies it can cause weight loss and a 'failure to thrive'.

Babies have a tendency to reflux because:

- Babies have small stomachs
- Babies spend a lot of their time in a lying position
- Babies are fed a mostly fluid diet. (Milk can easily come up, particularly with a burp.)
- Handling, such as nappy changing and bouncing, can increase the pressure on a baby's full tummy, which then increases the risk of reflux

What happens?

Food is supposed to travel in one direction through your body, down the oesophagus, into the stomach and through the bowel. But in a little one who suffers with reflux, there is a weakness in the band of muscles in the lower oesophagus. These join the stomach, acting as a valve. If this valve doesn't shut properly, milk can travel back up, resulting in your baby vomiting, which is called active reflux, or having a heartburn type of sensation, which is called silent reflux.

What are the symptoms?

If your baby has reflux, you might notice that they regurgitate a little milk that looks like cottage cheese after feeding. This can also cause discomfort in their oesophagus and make them cough a little. Don't worry, as long as your baby is otherwise well and healthy, they'll be fine. You just need to keep a cloth or tissue handy for catching their milk spills.

In some cases, where reflux symptoms are bad, you might want to speak to your midwife or health visitor about treatment. The symptoms of a more serious issue include:

- Reflux is happening more than five times a day on a regular basis

- Your baby cries excessively after feeds
- Your baby vomits regularly
- Coughing becomes a regular occurrence

How do you treat Reflux?

Try feeding your baby in an upright position or holding them for 20 minutes after feeds, this really helped my two to settle after their dream feeds. You could also experiment with smaller but more frequent feeds first or raise the head end of your baby's cot or crib slightly to help them sleep. If the symptoms persist you should visit your doctor, who might prescribe infant Gaviscon or, in extreme cases, Ranitidine.

Infant Gaviscon works by mixing with the stomach contents, stabilising and thickening them to reduce the reflux symptoms and frequency. It's an easily administered powder and comes in one-dose sachets.

Ranitidine works by reducing the amount of stomach acid produced and thus prevents reflux causing inflammation in the oesophagus. It also allows existing inflammation to heal. However, it does not decrease the amount of spilling or vomiting and it could take anything from a few days to a few weeks to see an improvement in your child's condition after starting Ranitidine.

Although Ranitidine syrup contains ethanol, which is a form of alcohol, and was not formulated for paediatric use, it has been used successfully in the treatment of reflux in children for many years.

While the infant Gaviscon worked for Betsy, it didn't even touch the edges of pain for Oscar and he was eventually prescribed Ranitidine. In his case we were very lucky and, after only 24 hours, noticed a huge difference. The little man went from unhappy chappy to contented little nappy very quickly.

Luckily for us, Betsy grew out of her reflux when she was four months old and was gradually weaned off the Gaviscon. Reflux symptoms tend to gradually disappear with time as your baby's digestive system matures.

For most babies spitting up will have decreased remarkably by the age of five or six months and disappears completely by the age of twelve months. But in severe cases it may persist for up to 18 months.

If you think your baby might be suffering with reflux, talk to your health visitor or GP as soon as you can. Don't wait or worry you might be wrong, it's better to get these things checked sooner rather than later.

If your baby is diagnosed with reflux, try not to worry. You're not alone in your suffering! As many as one in three babies suffer with some form of reflux in the early days. So, when you're pacing the room at night with your little bundle crying, just think to yourself, "It will get better soon, and there's a million other parents pacing the room tonight too!"

Eczema

My two littlies have mild eczema and in the winter months it can get quite sore and often lead to night waking.

Eczema is a inflammatory condition of the skin that causes redness, dryness, scaling and itching. It leaves little ones very unhappy and parents exhausted as flare ups can cause unsettled night-times.

Eczema is commonly seen in young children before the age of five, although it can appear anytime throughout childhood. Eczema is a long-term, or chronic, condition, but in most cases it disappears before adulthood. It can be mild or severe and symptoms may come and go.

The basic treatment for eczema is founded on avoiding things that irritate the skin. This can include certain foods, or in young babies certain formula milks. It has been suggested that exclusively breast feeding for six months can reduce the chances of getting eczema quite considerably.

Moisturising your little one frequently will lessen the dryness. If the eczema is particularly bad, your doctor might prescribe oral or topical antibiotics.

Teething

M ost babies get their first baby tooth, otherwise known as milk tooth, at around six months, usually in the front and at the bottom. However, all babies are different. Mine got their little teeth in a topsy-turvy order and didn't get all of them until they were eleven months old! Betsy cut her first nine in one go!

Some babies are even born with teeth and others still have no teeth on their first birthday! However, as a guideline, most babies will have all their milk teeth by the time they are two and a half.

How many teeth?

T here are 20 primary teeth; ten in the top row and ten at the bottom. Your child's first permanent adult teeth will grow, normally at the back, at around five or six years old - after the milk teeth fall out and the tooth fairy replaces them with coins. But don't worry, the gappy years make for such fab photos!

Symptoms of teething

I t's not as easy as you would expect to diagnose that disturbed sleep as the result of teething. The symptoms you should look out for include:

- Red cheeks
- Runny nappies
- Sore bottom
- Dribbling
- Everything goes into little-ones' mouth (chewing lots)
- Temperature
- Disturbed sleep

Teething is a pain

The majority of babies suffer with teething; usually during the night when the pain easily distracts them from sleep. Some babies don't suffer at all, but I've yet to meet a parent who's little one didn't suffer while cutting at least one of their teeth.

Don't panic - teething pain is normal and there are lots of remedies available. There are also lots of things you can do to comfort your little one through the teething times!

Give your baby something hard to chew on, such as a teething toy, a breadstick, or even a peeled carrot. Always remember though; supervise children with food in case of choking – don't give them teething toys or food and leave them along to go to sleep!

You should also avoid encouraging constant chewing and

sucking on sugary things as this can cause tooth decay.

Littlies with gummy smiles

If your baby is over four months old, you can rub sugar-free teething gel on their gums, which works briefly, or teething powders which are my personal favourite and last much longer.

If your littly is really suffering, you can try some infant paracetamol or ibuprofen. But always remember to follow the instructions on the bottle for your child's age. And always check with you pharmacist that it's suitable for your baby.

Teething and nappies

Use a barrier cream on their little bottoms as runny nappies are common during teething. You should also avoid too much acidic fruit, which can aggravate sore tummies when teething.

Finally, buy a baby toothbrush and brush those new teeth as soon as they appear!

Unfortunately, with teething, routines go out of the window so avoid any sleep training techniques and instead apply lots of love, cuddles and TLC when needed.

Colds and flu

During the winter months it's highly likely your littlies will get a cold. Mine do, without fail, and I have to say I dread the sleepless nights, snotty noses and unhappy poppets that go hand in hand with a cold.

Colds and flu are caused by viruses. (How I hate viruses!) Did you know that there are more than 200 common cold viruses, and three types of flu virus? So, you see, avoiding a cold is pretty difficult!

These viruses are spread through droplets that are coughed and sneezed out by an infected person, and spread through the air or via your hands. If you have a cold and you touch your nose or eyes and then touch someone else, you may pass the virus on to them.

Symptoms

You probably know the symptoms of colds, but if you are lucky enough to have never suffered (what's your secret?) here they are:

- Coughing
- Sore throat
- Sneezing

- Blocked nose
- Headache
- Slight temperature

Treatment

Unfortunately, with colds, there isn't really anything your doctor can do to treat them. The best thing to do is visit your local pharmacy where you can get advice on how to manage the symptoms and buy over-the-counter medicine.

With children's medicines its really important to seek the advice of a pharmacist rather than guess! Some over the counter medicines are very strong for little people. It's important to say here that aspirin should NOT be given to children under 26 months old.

As always, when giving your child medicine, check the dosage on the side of the carton and keep for future reference.

You should also consider alternatives to medicine, such as warm, home-made honey and lemon drinks for older children, removing layers of clothing if little ones are hot and making sure you keep their fluids up.

You may find that, when your little one has a cold, they don't want to eat big meals. Give them little amounts of food often and encourage them to eat fruits that are high in Vitamin C.

You should keep your child warm and comfortable and make sure they are well rested. If you are worried that their cold is developing into something else, such as a high fever, dad cough or flu, take them along to see your GP.

All babies under three months with a temperature of more than 38°C (100.4°F) should be urgently assessed by a doctor, as should babies aged three to six months with a temperature higher than 39°C (102.2°F).

As with any illness, routines go out of the window so avoid sleep training techniques and give lots of love and kisses instead.

The norovirus

The norovirus, better known as the winter vomiting bug (or, in our house, the nasty sick sick bug) is the most common stomach bug in the UK, affecting people of all ages.

The norovirus is highly contagious so once one member of the family gets it, it's likely the rest of the family will too.

The norovirus causes vomiting and diarrhoea, which in turn can cause dehydration. As a result, as with any sickness bug, it's important to keep your littlies well hydrated. The best way of doing this is to give them frequent little sips of water. Even if they bring back the fluids, keep topping them up.

Treatment

There is no specific cure for Norovirus – you simply have to let it run its course. But it shouldn't last more than a couple of days. If your littlies get norovirus, follow these simple guidelines.

- Get them to drink plenty of water to avoid dehydration
- Give infant paracetamol for any fever or pain
- If your little one feels like eating, get them to eat foods that are easy to digest
- Stay at home and don't go to the doctor, because norovirus

is contagious and there is nothing the doctor can do while you have it. However, you may wish to visit your GP if symptoms last longer than a few days.

- Children who have an unusually high temperature or become lethargic should seek medical advice

To avoid spreading the virus, you should keep your child away from school or nursery for at least 48 hours after their last episode of diarrhoea or vomiting. Also, children should not swim in a swimming pool for two weeks following the last episode of diarrhoea.

> **Tummy bugs are no fun at all. Keep a close eye on your little one's temperature and behaviour. Keep them hydrated #FluidsLittleandOften**

NHS guide to dehydration

Diarrhoea and vomiting are more serious in babies than older children - because babies can easily lose too much fluid from their bodies and become dehydrated. They may become lethargic or irritable, have a dry mouth, and have loose, pale or mottled skin. Their eyes and fontanelle (the soft spot on the top of their head) may become sunken. Unfortunately for us, Betsy had to stay overnight in the children's ward after a nasty bout of norovirus led to dehydration.

If a child becomes dehydrated they may not pass much urine, lose their appetite and have cold hands and feet. It might be difficult to tell how much urine they're passing when they have diarrhoea.

If your baby becomes dehydrated they will need extra fluids. You can buy oral rehydration fluids from your local pharmacy or chemist, or get a prescription from your GP. Brands include Dioralyte, Electrolade and Rehydrate.

Contact your GP or health visitor urgently for advice if your baby has passed six or more diarrhoeal stools in the past 24 hours or if your baby has vomited three times or more in the same time frame. Get expert advice if your baby is very unwell. For example, if they are less responsive, feverish, are not passing much urine or if they have been vomiting for more than more than a day, get your GP's advice straightaway.

Again, sleep training techniques should be replaced with love, cuddles and tender, loving care.

Meningitis

Bacterial meningitis and septicaemia affect around 3,400 people in the UK each year, killing more children under the age of five than any other infectious disease. It is serogroup B (MenB), which is the root case of the majority of meningitis cases and deaths in the UK.

Meningitis should be treated as a medical emergency because bacterial meningitis can lead to septicaemia (blood poisoning), which can be fatal.

Bacterial meningitis is the more serious form of the condition. The symptoms usually begin suddenly and rapidly get worse. If you suspect a case of bacterial meningitis, you should phone 999 immediately to request an ambulance.

There are some early warning signs that you may notice before the other symptoms appear.

Early warning signs

Bacterial meningitis has a number of early warning signs that can occur earlier than the other symptoms. These are:

- Pain in the muscles, joints or limbs, such as the legs or hands

- Unusually cold hands and feet, or shivering
- Pale or blotchy skin and blue lips
- The presence of a high temperature (fever) plus any of the above symptoms should be taken very seriously. Phone 999 immediately to request an ambulance.

Early symptoms

The early symptoms of bacterial meningitis are similar to those of many other conditions, and include:

- A severe headache
- Fever
- Nause and vomiting
- Feeling generally unwell

Late onset symptoms

As the condition gets worse it may cause:

- Drowsiness
- Confusion
- Seizures or fits
- Photophobia, or the inability to tolerate bright lights. This is less common in young children

- A stiff neck – also less common in young children
- Rapid breathing
- A blotchy red rash that does not fade or change colour when you place a glass against it – the rash is not always present

Babies and young children

The symptoms of bacterial meningitis are different in babies and young children. Possible symptoms include:

- Becoming floppy and unresponsive or stiff with jerky movements
- Becoming irritable and not wanting to be held
- Unusual crying
- Vomiting and refusing feeds
- Pale and blotchy skin
- Loss of appetite
- Staring expression
- Very sleepy with a reluctance to wake up
- Some babies will develop a swelling in the soft part of their head (fontanelle)

Viral meningitis

Most people with viral meningitis will have mild flu-like symptoms, such as:

- Headaches
- Fever
- Generally not feeling very well

In more severe cases of viral meningitis symptoms may include:

- Neck stiffness
- Muscle or joint pain
- Nausea
- Vomiting
- Diarrhoea
- Photophobia

Finally, unlike bacterial meningitis, viral meningitis does not usually lead to septicaemia.

Meningitis can strike quickly and without warning. If you suspect your little one has Meningitis don't hang about. Seek medical attention as soon as possible #Meningitis

Tonsillitis

Tonsillitis is the inflammation of the tonsils – which are the ball shaped bits at the back of the throat. It is usually caused by a viral infection or, less commonly, a bacterial infection. It is very common in children aged five to 15 years old. Almost all children will have at least one episode of tonsillitis as they grow up!

Symptoms

- Sore throat that can feel worse when swallowing
- High temperature (fever) over 38°C (100.4°F)
- Coughing
- Headache
- Tonsillitis is not usually a serious condition but your little one will feel unwell and uncomfortable for around three or four days

You will only need to visit the doctor if your child has symptoms lasting longer than four days that show no signs of improvement or they have more severe symptoms, such as being unable to eat or drink because of their pain, or having breathing breathing difficulties.

Tonsillitis can spread easily, so it's important to keep your child away from school or nursery until your GP says it is safe for them to return. This is usually when their symptoms have passed.

You should encourage your child to wash their hands before eating and after coughing and sneezing to avoid spreading the infection.

Treatment

There is no specific treatment for tonsillitis, but there are several things that can help alleviate symptoms, such as:

- Paracetamol or ibuprofen to help relieve pain
- Plenty of bed rest
- Encouraging your child to drink plenty of fluids

Your child may not feel like eating, so give them foods that are easy to swallow such a soups, jelly, rice pudding and, my favourite for poorly poppets, ice-cream! Again, avoid sleep training techniques and opt for love and cuddles.

Chickenpox

Chickenpox is a common childhood illness that most littlies catch at some point in their lives. However, it is more common under the age of ten years old.

We haven't had the delights of chickenpox yet in our household and, to be honest, I'm not looking forward to it as I've dealt with so many cases over the years. It's no fun!

Although its considered to be a mild illness, you can expect your child to feel pretty poorly and miserable during their chickenpox days.

There is no need to see your GP, unless your child's temperature hits the heights I've described earlier. However, as before, if you recognise the signs and spots of chickenpox and think your child is very unwell, for example if they have infected spots, an unusually high temperature or difficulty breathing you might want to head on over the the GP's surgery, contact NHS Direct or even, in the case of difficulty breathing, head to casualty.

Symptoms

The symptoms of chickenpox include a temperature and a rash of red, itchy spots that quickly turn into fluid-filled blisters. They look unpleasant and can cause lots of discomfort to little ones.

The original blisters eventually crust over to form scabs, which ultimately drop off. Chickenpox is most infectious from one to two days before the rash starts and until all the blisters have crusted over, which is usually five to six days after the start of the rash.

Some children have only a few spots, but some unlucky poppets get them all over body and sometimes in not-so-nice places as well!

However, Chickenpox spots are *most* likely to appear on the face, ears and scalp, under the arms, on the chest and stomach and on the arms and legs. But occasionally they can be found inside the ear on the genitals and up the nose . Ouch!

If your little one has Chickenpox try to:

- Prevent spreading the infection by keeping them off nursery or school until ALL the spots have crusted over
- Keep them away from public areas to avoid contact with people who have not had it, especially people who are at risk of serious problems, such as newborn babies, pregnant women and anyone with a weakened immune system (for example, people having cancer treatment or taking steroid tablets)

Treatment

There is no specific treatment for Chickenpox, but there are lots of tips and advice available. Some of these you'll get even if you don't ask for them!

During my career I've been through many bouts of Chickenpox with littlies and have to say that, above all other treatments I've found sudocrem works wonders, combined with Piriton, if they are over twelve months old, which reduces swelling and irritation. However, doctors can prescribe Piriton for babies over a month old, but you should never take this initiative yourself.

Top tips for fighting nasty spots

- Keep nails short
- Dress your littly in soft clothes (cotton PJs are great!)
- Use non-drying lotions and creams (Sudocrem is fab for this!)

There are many pharmacy remedies which can alleviate symptoms, such as infant paracetamol to relieve fever, and lotions, creams and cooling gels to ease the horrid itching.

Don't forget to ask other parents what worked best for them! Some home remedies, such as the famous oatmeal bath, work but all littlies are different, so it's really just a case of experimenting to see what makes your little one the most comfortable.

When to see the doctor

Contact your GP straight away if your child develops any abnormal symptoms, for example:

- If the blisters on their skin become infected
- If your child has a pain in their chest or has difficulty breathing

Immunisations

The majority of babies and children have no side effects at all after having immunisations and for those that do, any side effects tend to be mild and last only a short time. Having said that, it can cause a disruption to sleep so it is something to be prepared for if your little one is due to have theirs.

The most common reactions include:

- Swelling, redness and sensitivity around the injection site, a mild fever, diarrhoea, crying, irritability, drowsiness, and going off their milk or food
- If you are at all concerned after an injection - contact your doctor or health visitor

I'd advise that whenever your child is feeling unsettled due to immunisations give them lots of cuddles and ride it through for a night or two. You can give infant paracetamol for pain or fever, but remember to always check the dosage and age for your child. It's only for babies and children aged from two months, weighing more than 4kg and not born prematurely.

As with any disruptions to the regular happy baby bedtime - get back into your routine as soon as they are feeling better.

Finally, with the majority of common childhood illnesses, try not to worry. Recovery happens and they'll soon be back to their old selves!

> **When little ones are poorly or teething don't worry about routines and don't use sleep training techniques.**
> **#PoorlyPoppetsNeedCuddles**

CHAPTER 14

WEANING PLANS AND ROUTINES

Weaning can be both an exciting and worrying time for any parent. Even if you've done it before, it's so easy to forget how you did it and anyway, things may have changed!

Some childcare experts say weaning should start at around six months old, or even later, but in my experiences both as a professional nanny and as a mum, I've found that the littlies in my care, including my own son and daughter were hungry and more than ready to make a start at around four-five months old. Some people think that starting solid foods before six months will help a baby sleep, but there is no evidence to support this. Go by your own baby's needs and your instinct - as a parent you will know when your child is ready.

That said, if your baby was premature, talk to your health visitor or GP about the right age to start your baby on solid foods.

My four week weaning plan is very simple and you can adapt it to suit your baby's needs. It also leads on and fits well with the *Fi's Four for Happiness* routine, so I've built that into the weaning routine. It's just a guide though, of course you don't have to do all the activities suggested! Your day is yours and our baby's to have fun with as you please.

Remember this is only a guide. Your baby may need more or less milk than suggested. Observe your baby; watch them at each step. Do they still seem hungry after they have had their meal? Are they full and rejecting more food? Do they turn their head or refuse to open their mouth? Go by their lead.

Adapt the following plan to suit your times. This plan is based on the *Fi's Four for Happiness* routine, which uses the times six am/ten am/two pm/six pm/two am, which is four hourly feeds. As I've explained, the two am feed is usually cut between eight and twelve weeks, depending on baby.

Weaning plan: week one

6am: Feed given as usual, followed by baby porridge made up with a little of baby's milk. Baby porridge is less bland than baby rice! Have you ever tasted baby rice? It's not pleasant and *so* dull. Porridge has a much nicer consistency.

Next you should clean baby up after the, inevitably, messy start to the day, then pop them down for a morning nap. Get ready for the day yourself now, and make sure you've had breakfast!

10am: Feed as usual, wind and change

10.30am: Activity time; go for walk or perhaps have a go at one of our play ideas! Whatever you decide to do, try and stick closely to the routine.

12.30pm: Nap time

Change baby so they are fresh for nap time then pop the little one into bed for a sleep.

2pm: Feed as usual

Afternoon activity

5pm: Bath time, followed by PJs, a story or some singing and ready for feed

6pm: Feed as usual

Continue this all week. You may notice towards the end of the week that the 10am feed is being rejected or very little is being taken. This is fine.

Week two

Continue the daily routine and nap times as in week one

6am: Feed as normal, followed by baby porridge but now increase the portion size a little

10am: Offer the feed as usual, but it may be rejected. This is good!

12pm lunch: Offer pureed vegetables or fruit (there are a few ideas on the weaning page)

2pm: Feed as usual - this may be rejected or only a little taken - this is fine!

6pm: Feed as usual

Continue this all week. You may notice towards the end of the week that the 10am feed is being rejected every time. It is now OK to drop this feed but don't drop the 2pm feed just yet.

Week three

6am: Feed as usual, followed by baby porridge

10am: This feed should now be dropped and a snack offered instead. Try cool, boiled water and finger foods or fruit such as banana. Remember to supervise your baby at all times with finger foods to avoid choking.

12pm: For lunch, offer your little one pureed vegetables or fruit and boiled water. Again, there are a few ideas later. Increase the portion size.

2pm: Feed as usual – this may be rejected now and that's fine.

6pm: Feed as usual

Continue this all week. You may notice towards the end of the week that the 2pm feed is being rejected or very little is being taken. This is good.

Week four

6am: Feed your baby as normal and then try some more baby porridge. I know it seems dull, but it's what your baby needs for now!

10am: Offer baby a snack, again: cool boiled water and finger foods or fruit such as banana are ideal.

12pm lunch: Now the 2pm feed comes forward to lunchtime! Give baby their feed, followed by pureed vegetables or fruit.

2pm: Feed now dropped. You can have a cup of tea and a play with baby instead!

3.30/4pm: Prepare baby a tea of pureed vegetables or fruit and cool boiled water

6pm: Feed as usual

Continue this all week and then, congratulations, your baby will now be fully weaned!

Points to remember

Don't worry if your baby doesn't want to drop feeds – it's OK! Milk is an essential part of a baby's diet so don't force them to stop. Let your baby be your guide. If they are rejecting the feed, or taking very little, this means they are ready to cut that feed.

You don't have to complete the plan in four weeks. It's not a race and should be fun! If you feel your baby needs longer to adjust, simply extend to eight weeks and follow week one twice, week two twice and so on. It's all about having fun and enjoying the experience.

Then, once weaning is established, vary the food. But don't get too crazy too quickly. Babies have delicate palates and this is a new thing they are going through. There is plenty of time to experiment with food!

Don't stress! Enjoy! This is an important and special time. Enjoy every minute of it and take lots of messy photos!

> **Weaning is a fun time for you and your little one. Enjoy the mess and once weaning is established encourage a variety of foods and tastes #WeaningisFun!**

What to feed your baby

Here are a few first weaning recipes for you to try that my two really enjoyed!

Sweet potato, broccoli and basilicious

You'll need: One sweet potato, five or six leaves of fresh basil, five or six chopped broccoli florets.

Method: Steam or boil the vegetables, then blend them together with a little of your baby's milk and the chopped basil until smooth.

Butternut squash with minted peas

You'll need: Butternut squash, peas, four fresh mint leaves

Method: Boil or steam the squash and the peas until tender then blend with a little of baby's milk and the fresh mint until smooth.

Jack's vegetable winter warmer

You'll need: One parsnip, one carrot, one small swede, one small sweet potato

Method: Peel and chop all the vegetables, place in a pan, cover with water and simmer for 25 to 30 minutes, until all the vegetables are soft. Then drain the vegetables, reserving the cooking liquid, mash or puree, adding the reserved liquid or a little of baby's milk to obtain the required consistency.

Benjamin Bunny's allotment puree

You'll need: Three carrots, peeled and diced, three parsnips, peeled and diced

Method: Steam the vegetables until they're tender. Purée in a blender and adjust the texture with boiled cooled water or baby's usual milk.

CHAPTER 15

COMFORTERS

As many parents know, comforters are a big part of childhood, so I think it's important to include them in my baby bedtime book. Studies have shown that little ones who use comforters are significantly more likely to sleep through the night than those with no comforter.

In 'Children's choice of comforters and their effects on sleep' J Adkin argues that of the children using the comforters classified as 'easy access' (i.e. comforters they were more likely to find and hold), 71% were sleeping through the night at six months old. The associations were incremental, in that of those children who used both 'easy access' comforters and comforters requiring parental input, 48% were sleeping through the night at six months. And of those children using only parental input comforters, only 38%

were sleeping through the night.

It makes sense really doesn't it? When your little one forms an attachment to something, and has that something with them when they are in bed, it helps them get back to sleep by providing the reassurance they need during those light sleep phases. Remember, that's the most common time for babies to wake up!

Not only do comforters help as a sleep aid, they also help reassure little ones going through stressful situations such as starting a nursery, a doctor's visit or a stay away from home.

Choosing a comforter

You'll often find a child's comforter is something that was a gift from a friend or family member, or a blanket that is, or was, used regularly. You can also buy purpose made comforters such as taggy blankets or popular comforters like little baby soft toys.

If you'd like introduce a comforter, I'd suggest choosing something that is safety standards tested, soft to the touch and small enough to pack. And it should most definitely be machine washable! I'd also suggest investing in two or three identical comforters, just to be safe, to make washing the comforter easier or to compensate if one becomes lost. Then the end of the world wont be the end of the world!

> **Not only do comforters help as a sleep aid, they also help little ones going through stressful situations #TeddyBearFriend**

Losing beloved comforters can cause all kinds of unhappy nights, as I very nearly found out one holiday. You'd have thought that, after all my years of working with little ones, when my own two became attached to certain things I'd have bought spares? No.

On a holiday to Turkey, Betsy's beloved Rabbit got lost. Well, I say lost. He got taken!

Poor Rabbit was minding his own business in our room on Betsy's bed when in came the cleaners, swept him up in the laundry pile and off he went, never to be seen again. The hotel were terribly apologetic, they sent out a rabbit search party and notified their other hotels and laundry departments, but by the end of our holiday Rabbit was still missing.

Thankfully, Betsy took this all very calmly, probably because she has more than one comforter. (She has Moo Cow and Rosie doll too!) She was also having a wonderful holiday and so we told her that Rabbit had decided to stay on in Turkey and would return later, which she thought was fun.

I did eventually find a replacement rabbit - but the only one I could find was bigger. So we told her that Rabbit had overindulged on Turkish Delights!

Oscar snuggles a blue star fleece blanket and sucks his thumb. I now have four of these blankets as I'm not taking chances again! This means I get to wash them without him realising and if we ever lose one there are spares!

Whatever comforter you decide to use, or your child attaches themselves to, try and use them for bedtimes only. My two keep theirs on their bed, but if they are unwell, or a little worried about something, I let them have their comforters to reassure them.

Ditching the dummy

I don't think it matters really how long children have comforters. I'll even admit to still having my teddy bear on my bed. It's really no big deal at all, but with dummies it's a little different.

Many paediatricians and speech therapists say that twelve months is a good time to wean your child off a dummy because this marks the beginning of a spurt in language development. I'd suggest that if you are using a dummy - always use it for naps and bedtimes rather than during the day - especially with older babies and young toddlers who are starting to talk.

Sometimes dummies can cause your little one's upper teeth to tip forward toward the lip. Having said that, try not to worry as they usually return to normal after a few dummy free months. The bigger concern is their big teeth, the permanent adult teeth, that come through once your little one has lost their baby teeth. This usually happens at around five or six years old, so it's advisable to ditch the dummy well before that time!

As a mum of two little ones I know how important a good night's sleep is and so the thought of getting rid of something that soothes your little one to sleep can be quite daunting!

I was so worried about ditching the dummy with Betsy, as I'm used to sleeping well and not having to worry that my littlies are unhappy or unsettled, that I did the worst possible thing and put it off.

From my own experience I'd advise ditching the dummy as soon as you can. It is a great comforter and really helps little ones but, the longer they have one, the harder it is to let go.

For me, I used any excuse to make the weeks go by, 'she's not well' or 'she's teething' – anything I could think of to delay tears at bedtime and avoid having an upset little girl in the night, when she couldn't find her dummy.

I really should've given my little girl more credit.

We gave up dummies in one night, and we didn't have had one teary moment, one upset bedtime, one disturbed night or any mention of buying more!

How did I do it?

There are lots of ways of ditching the dummy. You can do it gradually over time, or get creative and do it in one go, by inventing stories that the dummy fairy has taken it. Or you can swap the dummies for something more exciting, like a new toy or new comforter.

For me it was a risk, but I just went for it. I took every dummy from the house and put them in the bin. I had one spare, just in case it all went a little crazy that night.

At bedtime Betsy had her usual bath, milk and story and climbed into bed. She settled down and felt around for her dummies which were usually under her pillow.

Gone.

"Oh no! mummy!" she said. "My dummies!" (she had three!) "My dummies, they're gone!"

Enter my very fabulous acting skills; "What? They have? Let me see!"

I looked under the pillow and around the bed, in cupboards and drawers.

"They *have* disappeared!"

No tears, just laughing, smiling and discussing where they could possibly have gone. We talked about them perhaps going to a new baby somewhere, or perhaps they'd gone on a dummy holiday?

"Oh well, never mind," said I, hoping the tears wouldn't come. Very calm. Very matter of fact, And then I snuggled her down for the night.

And you know what? The tears didn't come. All that came was, "Oh well, never mind!" And a little girl snuggled her bunny and went to sleep.

Simple.

Now I know this sounds like it could be pot luck, but I've suggested this technique to the hundreds of parents who have come to me asking how to get rid of the dummies? And it's worked. Time and time again.

A week later, we talked about the dummies, but only when she brought it up. We said how we wondered where they went. Did they perhaps go on holiday? Were they perhaps too babyish for her and so went to find a baby? Each time we talked, she didn't get upset and she didn't ask for another one.

The important thing to remember when ditching the dummy is that, even though it is a big deal – don't make a big deal out of it.

Whichever way you decide to ditch the dummy, don't make it a drama. Little ones catch on very quickly if something is wrong because of they way you act. If you behave calmly and matter of factly about the situation they will respond, in the majority of cases, in the same way.

> **Don't make a big deal out of ditching the dummy – even if it is a big deal. Little ones follow your lead #DitchTheDummyPositively**

CHAPTER 16

FINAL THOUGHTS BEFORE BED

As a nursery nurse, and as a nanny, I knew that children were hard work. But I also knew they were incredible fun. I learned very quickly that, because children grow so fast we should love each day with them.

Being a parent is both challenging and incredibly rewarding. It's often tiring, frustrating and emotional, but the wonderful, fun and happy memories make all the hard times worth it. All the sleepless nights become a distant memory and all the dirty nappies and sickness become a speck of dust in a pile of wonderful memories.

If I have one final piece of advice, it would be to enjoy every moment with your little one because they grow so fast.

Love each day – even when those days that have followed a sleepless night.

And you will have bad nights – even the best sleepers keep their parents awake some nights - but that's just part and parcel of being a parent.

Don't sweat the small stuff – the washing can wait, a take-away once in a while when you're shattered really doesn't matter – what's important is time with your little ones. Enjoy each moment and love each day.

I hope that by helping you to have a happy bedtime baby, you can enjoy every single precious waking moment with your little one, instead of feeling tired and desperate. And that like me, you'll enjoy going into their room to watch them sleep peacefully.

The baby bedtime book – say goodnight to sleepless nights.

REFERENCES

Website references

NHS www.nhs.uk

SIDS, The Lullaby trust www.lullabytrust.org.uk

Noah – Spina Bifida and Hydrocephalus awareness www.hugsforNoah.co.uk

Journal Reference

*Han-Seok Seo et al. Effects of Coffee Bean Aroma on the Rat Brain Stressed by Sleep Deprivation: A Selected Transcript- and

2D Gel-Based Proteome Analysis. Journal of Agricultural and Food Chemistry, June 25, 2008

Photography

Front cover photograph of Baby Ollie by Jay Emme – Jay Emme Photography www.jayemmephotography.co.uk